Musings of a
Baby Boomer

Musings
of a
Baby Boomer

Life Before X, Y, and Z

Happy Musings!

Kay Hoflander

Kay Hoflander

BROWN BOOKS
PUBLISHING GROUP

Musings of a Baby Boomer
Life Before X, Y, and Z

Brown Books Publishing Group
Dallas, TX / New York, NY
www.BrownBooks.com
(972) 381-0009

A New Era in Publishing®

Names: Hoflander, Kay, author.

Title: Musings of a baby boomer : life before X, Y, and Z / Kay Hoflander.
Description: Dallas, TX ; New York, NY : Brown Books Publishing Group, [2022]
   | A collection of selected shorts from Hoflander's weekly newspaper column
   "Full Circle." | Includes bibliographical references.
Identifiers: ISBN 9781612545455 (hardcover) | ISBN 9781612545462 (ebook)
Subjects: LCSH: Baby boom generation--Humor. | Aging--Humor. | Technolo-
   gy--Humor. | Life--Humor. | LCGFT: Humor.
Classification: LCC PN6231.B22 H64 2022 (print) | LCC PN6231.B22 (ebook)
   | DDC 818.602--dc23

ISBN 978-1-61254-545-5
LCCN 2021922405

Printed in the United States
10 9 8 7 6 5 4 3 2 1

For more information or to contact the author, please go to
www.KayHoflander.com.

To anyone who comes to this unexpected epiphany:
"I'm the same inside! This is the big secret! You will
always be you no matter how old you are."
Happy reading!

Table of Contents

Patriotism and Politics

Family and Friends

The Joy of Technology

Summers Past

Wisdom of Experience

Preface

---

*"Youth is not a time of life; it is a state of mind . . . Whether
sixty or sixteen, there is in every human being's heart the lure of
wonder, the unfailing childlike appetite of what's next and the joy of
the game of living. In the center of your heart and my heart there is a
wireless station: so long as it receives messages of beauty, hope, cheer,
courage, and power from men and from the Infinite, so long are you
young. When the aerials are down, and your spirit is covered with
snows of cynicism and the ice of pessimism, then you are grown old,
even at twenty, but as long as your aerials are up, to catch waves
of optimism, there is hope you may die young at eighty."*

—SAMUEL ULLMAN, an American businessman, poet, and
humanitarian, born in Germany in 1840 and immigrated
with his family to the United States in 1851

"Full Circle" was the title of a newspaper column I wrote from 2005
to 2012, seven years of weekly columns centered around the reluctant
aging of the baby boomer generation, my generation. Baby boomers
were often dubbed the generation that behaved differently than those
before it, perhaps paving the way for those generations who have come
since—X, Y, Z, and so on.

My generational experience inspired a wide range of column
topics. The chapter titles of this book reflect these topics—Rites of
Passage, remembering Happy Boomer Days, Family and Friends,
Patriotism and Politics, The Joy (or not) of Technology, the sweet
nostalgia of Summers Past, and the Wisdom of Experience.

To my surprise, readers seemed to react exactly as I did to the stories
and tales I recalled and wrote about each week in the newspaper. Their
comments were uplifting and convinced me that my experiences are
indeed universal among those of my generation. One of my favorite

comments from a reader was this: "Your articles are like emotional B-12 shots to the psyche!"

I understand that when I wrote these, my then college-age and twenty-something kids may not have grasped all the nuances of which I speak—but my baby boomer peers did. My hope is that you, dear readers, will as well. More than that, I hope that my children and grandchildren and yours (Generations X, Y, Z, and beyond) will better understand baby boomers, those born between 1946 and 1964.

Two tips for the reader:

1. Keep in mind, these columns were written "live." Although in my day one did not typically say something was "live," we more likely said "in real time." For example, a column titled "A Complicated Relationship with GPS" was published in the newspaper on April 26, 2012. In that real time, everything about a GPS was complicated and foreign to us. Today, that would not be true, of course, and it would be comical to think the original GPS was difficult to learn and use.

2. This is not necessarily a book to read from front to back, although it will work just fine that way. It may be better enjoyed by randomly choosing a chapter or column, or by starting at the back and working forward.

Above all else, I hope these short columns remind you, dear readers, that humor is to be found in all areas of life; never cease to look for it!

Kay Hoflander

Kay Hoflander

P.S. There are more than seventy columns in this book, but over the seven years that I wrote my weekly newspaper column, the total number of stories topped three hundred. That's a lot of stories. Topics, such as Animals, Weather and Seasons, Food and Recipes, Music, Television and Books, and Sports could make for a hearty sequel. We will see. In the meantime, happy reading!

Rites
of
Passage

"Two senior portions please."

Trying to Remember to Remember

"I always have trouble remembering three things: faces, names, and I can't remember what the third thing is."

—FRED ALLEN

The other day I went to the post office for stamps. I wanted those new ones, the ones that have the same price for years to come even if the US Postal Service raises postage rates ten years from now.

So, without a doubt in my mind as to the name of the stamps, I placed my order, "I would like a book of Timeless Stamps."

To which the clerk replied, "Sure, I know what you want, but you mean to say Forever Stamps don't you?"

Oh my. I did mean to say Forever Stamps but could not retrieve the name. The great part is that the clerk, who had to be pushing sixty, knew exactly what I intended to say. Bless him.

As I opened my mail at the tall worktable in the lobby of the post office, I sorted through the ads, flyers, and sundry junk mail. An advertising brochure for a name department store caught my eye. In it were samples of the latest men's and women's colognes. You know the flyers, the ones that have the scented side panels.

So, I stood there sniffing for some time and put the men's aftershave and cologne fragrances in one pile and the women's in another. Some were not to my liking, so I put them in the discard pile. The others I thought I probably should keep in case I wanted to buy one and could not remember the name. I stuck those into my computer/tote bag.

Time to leave, so off I went to finish my errands.

At the wireless coffee shop that afternoon I pulled out my computer, only to find my junk mail discard pile from earlier in the day. Not only was the entire lot of trash in there but so were the fragrance samples I wanted to keep.

There are no words to describe the jumble of smells that now reside in my tote bag. My computer even smells.

I could have sworn I threw those in the trash at the post office.

Groan.

The very next day my husband called me from work and said, "I forgot. I was supposed to remind you this morning. You told me last night to be sure and remind you at breakfast and I forgot before I left for work."

"Remind me of what?" I asked without a clue as to what I wanted to remember.

"Well, I don't know. I forgot," he said.

"So," I said, "Let me get this straight. You forgot what you were supposed to tell me in case I forgot."

"That's about it. I'll call you if I remember."

I hope we paid the light bill.

September 1, 2007

Medicare Birthday Alert: You Are Turning 65!

Letters advertising Medicare supplement insurance started to swamp our snail mailbox in the spring, just months before my husband would turn sixty-five in mid-August.

He did not want a birthday party, no gifts, no big deal made of his birthday; he certainly did not want to hear about Medicare.

Just let this milestone pass into oblivion, he insisted.

"I don't want to be reminded of my birthday," he reiterated. "It's already bad enough that I am the speed limit on US 50 Highway."

Whether he wanted it or not, an avalanche of Medicare letters deluged upon us all saying the same thing:

"Birthday alert. Birthday alert! Have you signed up for Medicare?" Technically speaking, signing up for Medicare is not mandatory, but good luck if you don't.

We wondered what he should do. What Medicare "Part" should he take? Part A? Part B? Part D?

"There are just too many 'Parts,'" hubby said.

Eventually, he acquiesced to the relentless direct mail pressure and trekked down to the closest Social Security office to sign up.

In truth, Medicare is really quite simple, according to the government. Here is an explanation of an abridged version:

If you have either or both Part A and Part B, you will need a Part D, that is unless you have a group plan already. If you do not get on a plan when first eligible you can only get on a plan from November 15 to December 31 of each year with an effective date of January 1. Then comes the penalty, 1 percent of the national average of all Part D plans for each month you are without it.

The penalties for Part B and Part D are permanent and will be added each month forever, so if you are eligible and delay it, that can add up to a lot of dollars.

Confused yet? We are, still.

And, to make a long story short, as the saying goes, the direct mail barrage did not stop long after hubby signed up for Medicare and a supplemental insurance plan.

Bored with too much information, he quit reading the mail and began throwing most of it in the trash, day after day.

To our surprise, about two weeks after he enrolled, we received a 10x12 official-looking packet of information from hubby's new supplemental insurance company. The letter referred to Part J insurance cards, his I.D. number, and how to use the Part J card.

You should have your Part J cards by now, the letter added. "What is Part J?" I asked, completely unfamiliar with the term.

"I don't know," the spousal unit agreed. "Oh yeah, I remember now. Some insurance cards came the other day that said Part J on them, but I thought it was a joke. Some sort of con. How many Parts can there be? So, I threw them away."

I think we might be starting over.

August 27, 2009

Class Reunion Anxiety Season Starts Now

*"The old dreams were good dreams.
They didn't work out, but I'm glad I had them."*[1]

—ROBERT KINCAID (CLINT EASTWOOD)
in *The Bridges of Madison County*, 1995

It is that time of year for class reunion anxiety, and I am starting to get a bad case of the jitters and heebie-jeebies.

What if I say something stupid at our upcoming class reunion?

I worry about this because I was visiting with a classmate about our imminent reunion recently, and I could not remember the answers to her questions.

Surely, old classmates won't think me too dimwitted if I can't remember exact details from our high school days. My recollections are more like fuzzy dreams, but good ones.

I do take comfort, however, in remembering what Ralph Waldo Emerson once said, "It is one of the blessings of old friends that you can afford to be stupid with them."

I emailed some old friends hoping they would remember the details I couldn't. I might need to know this in casual conversation at the reunion, I thought.

I was about to get stupid.

I wrote Robert: "I am trying to remember some things from our high school days. Just wondering, did I go to prom with you our junior year? My memory is not so good anymore."

"No, that would be Danny," he replied. "We never dated in high school, once in college."

"Oh," I answered sheepishly.

So, I asked, "Who did you take to prom then," to which he replied, "I don't remember."

I emailed Janet.

"Robert doesn't know who he took to prom our junior year. Do you remember?

"No," she wrote back with finality. "Why is this important?"

I called Beverly.

"No, I don't remember either, but I think you used to go with Steve to all the dances."

"I remember now," she said, "You two pretended to be a couple so Mr. Propes, our principal, would not charge you the rate for singles which was higher than for couples. You guys had a scam going. As soon as you were inside the door, you went your separate ways. It was a stroke of genius, actually. Don't you remember that?"

"If you say so," I replied, "But one more question. Did I go to Homecoming with Harvey once? I think I did. Paula says I did." I could hear Beverly sigh over the phone and tell me that it was probably better I didn't remember.

Now, my curiosity was killing me, so there was nothing to do but email Harvey.

"This is going to sound like a silly question, but did I go to Homecoming with you back in high school?"

"Yes, we dated once," he said matter of factly. "My mom drove us because neither of us were sixteen yet, and I got you a beautiful corsage, which you hated. You pouted; you wanted a Homecoming mum."

"Oh," I said, "So, who did you take to prom?" Harvey said he didn't remember.

I called my sister Pat.

"Well, let's see," she began with the brutal honesty only a sibling can provide.

"You had a date with Harvey for Homecoming, but his mother went along. You went with Steve, who was three years younger than you, to everything else but not really because you only did that to get in cheaper at the door. You went with your friend Danny to prom your junior year, and your senior year you went with a group of girls, but you really wanted to go with Ronnie. He didn't ask you."

I think I am going to stick with the old blurry dreams, the good ones. They didn't work out, but like Robert Kincaid, I'm glad I had them, too.

May 20, 2010

Mastering Online Dating at a Certain Age

Except perhaps in the world of online dating in which hundreds of thousands of singles are mastering this growing social phenomenon and becoming quite discerning in the process. They are getting good at it.

Those of us who are married have some difficulty understanding how this works, and we ask silly questions.

"Aren't you afraid? Don't people really just lie about their past?" Admittedly, we are often too free with our well-meaning advice, such as "Watch out for a con man who only wants your money" and "What if you attract a serial killer?"

This is not particularly supportive and helpful, I am told.

The main reason online dating is on my mind, however, is that I recently became aware of the large number of single people using these services, especially those of a certain age.

A lot.

But honestly, it is mind boggling to those of us not in the know.

So, I decided to learn more about online dating from my single friends.

Apparently, it can be a wild ride.

My friend Kat, for example, met a guy from Wyoming she dubbed WYO 2 because she was already chatting with another man from Wyoming, nicknamed WYO 1. All are in the over-sixty crowd.

WYO 2 wrote Kat an email for the first time beginning this way: "Dear Fat." What a way to start with a typo. "Kat" wrote back and said, "Yunno, in this early part of our relationship, I don't think you really need to be calling me names."

She was kidding.

Poor guy kept trying to explain himself and only made it worse.

Scratch WYO 2.

Back to WYO 1. By now they were at the telephoning stage of courtship. WYO 1 called Kat and wanted to meet. He told her he picked out three women from the online dating service and she was one of them. Whoopee, she thought.

"What am I, Door No. 1, 2, or 3?" she wondered.

Still, after getting over the urge to hit him, she decided this could be an intriguing encounter, so she agreed to meet him for coffee.

They talked for a couple of hours when he announced he had to go back to work, but would meet her for dinner later. When "later" came, he called saying he could not get away from work after all. That was OK with Kat because she already gave up on him and was now driving through Taco Bell, ordering her usual Friday night meat-and-cheese burrito with no sauce and no cheese, price $1.08.

The evening turned out just fine she decided, but she couldn't help wondering which one he was really with—Door No. 2 or 3.

Once she met a cattle rancher who lived thirty miles from the nearest town and could only be reached by satellite telephone.

Another time she met a man who used a picture that was at least ten years old on his profile page. He showed up for their first date in ugly shorts and horrid shirt packing fifty more pounds than in his online photo. She saw him arrive from the restaurant window and decided to stay and meet him even though he didn't look like his picture. She would've felt guilty canceling. Now as a seasoned online dating expert, she would call him on his cell and cancel before he ever set foot in the restaurant.

Yet another "match" drove six hours to meet her at a halfway point between their home cities. After coffee and a totally one-sided conversation about his son being on drugs, he announced that he had to leave because he had to work on his lawn mower.

Yes, it's a crazy online dating world, she admits, but offers some advice that is far better than my "watch out for serial killer" guidance. Kat says to look at it like a game, and then it's so much easier. If you happen to end up liking the person and they like you, then it's great.

That takes the pressure off knowing you are not committed to anything when you meet new people.

However, she gives one word of advice to senior men who are considering joining an online dating service. Kat says, "Don't let your grown daughter fill out your profile online for you. They just make up stuff they are not sure about, and meanwhile, the poor man has no idea he supposedly likes sushi."

So, Kat keeps at it.

After all, she says, you can't buy love on eBay.

April 29, 2010

Living to Be 100 and Moving to a Blue Zone

"The best age is the age you are."

—MAGGIE KUHN, founder of The Gray Panthers

Two friends emailed me recently on the same day with the same message, "Do you want to live to be one hundred or look and feel younger at every age?"

"OK, sure," I thought suspiciously, "but why are you asking? Do I need to look younger?" I don't think I want to know the answer to my own question.

"Take twenty minutes of your time and watch this video about Blue Zones," they each continued in lock step.

Since they are friends and they were asking, I decided to check out the website and Google search Blue Zones, wondering where or what in the world they were.

I soon learned that "where in the world" was the key point. Blue Zones are indeed geographic locations; places where climate and lifestyle can help you live to be a centenarian.

If I recall my geography studies from high school correctly, and that is a reach, there are temperate zones, frigid zones, and torrid zones in the world. But what are Blue Zones? I am sorry to admit that I never heard of them.

I know of Red Zones, Green Zones, Orange Zones, and Purple, but not Blue.

Red Zones are easy—the area between the 20-yard line and the goal line in football. If you are on defense, better keep your opponent out of the Red Zone.

The Green Zone was in the news for years—the international area protected by coalition forces inside the City of Baghdad.

Then, there is the Orange Zone. It has something to do with making calls abroad with one's mobile phone, but don't hold me to that. I suspect fans of Tennessee football would not agree with this definition since they have a completely different meaning for the term Orange Zone.

The Purple Zone was a funky 2006 comedy that few people watched, and it also refers to a football program at a small university in Texas, a newsletter, a store, a blog, and who knows what else.

But, back to Blue Zones.

People who live in these zones live longer and are reportedly happier and healthier than the rest of us. They do not get sick often and can function for many years without dementia or pain.

Here are the five (and there are only five) such spots that scientists believe offer health utopia: Sardinia, Italy; Islands of Okinawa, Japan; Loma Linda, California; Nicoya Peninsula, Costa Rica; and Icaria, Greece.

If I have to choose one of these Blue Zones, as my two email friends recommended, then I pick Sardinia, Italy, which sounds heavenly.

However, that was just until I learned that Sardinia's one-hundred year longevity principal only applies to males who live alone in mountain villages and eat goat cheese.

The other four locations weren't much different except for perhaps Loma Linda, and I have no idea why it is on the list.

My friends asked if I was ready to move to one of these Blue Zones because they were ready to relocate.

"No, absolutely not," I said remembering what Abraham Lincoln once said on the subject—"And in the end, it's not the years in your life that count. It's the life in your years."

But I might visit Loma Linda.

January 21, 2010

Become Bilingual—Stave off Alzheimer's?

*"It is possible at any age to discover a
lifelong desire you never knew you had."*

—ROBERT BRAULT

Did you ever want to learn a new language or brush up on one you used to know just for the fun of it? There might be a better reason than entertainment or personal enrichment to do just that.

The other day I was reading a magazine story that proclaimed a provocative idea: "stave off Alzheimer's, learn a second language."[2]

Indeed, new research is showing that one can benefit at any age from learning a new language. A quick web search provided numerous articles that backed up the theory that bilingual brains may delay mental aging.

Ellen Bialystok, a psychologist at York University in Toronto, says that studies are now revealing that advantages of bilingualism persist into old age, even as the brain's sharpness naturally declines. She suggests that bilingualism can "protect older adults from decline in the context of dementia."[3]

She adds that even if you don't learn a second language until after middle age, it can still help stave off dementia.

Outsmart Alzheimer's? "Could it be that easy?" I wondered.

Apparently, the idea is so appealing that folks over the age of fifty are stampeding to learn a foreign language.

On top of this trend themselves, my brother and sister-in-law called me recently to say they were ordering a French language software program. They thought it would be fun to learn and besides, they are retired and have a lot of time on their hands these days. If it staves off dementia, then all the better, they said.

I think I need to catch up.

Sure, like most baby boomers, I took a foreign language course in high school and can still read a little French, but I couldn't remember how to roll my r's if my life depended on it.

Deciding I should give my brain the exercise it needs, I chose to start afresh with a new language rather than brushing up on my forgotten French.

I chose Italian, but I'm not ordering any software. I know a little Italian from the movies.

Besides, Italian sounds easy to me, and I am already familiar with a few words and phrases: pizza, spaghetti, lasagna, risotto, panini.

Agreed, this is not exactly conjugating verbs, but I am betting, just like me, that you can follow this conversation in Italian that follows just fine, whether you think you can or not.

"Caio! Parli italiano?"

"Non capisco! Il mio italiano e orribile." "Come dite 'please' in italiano?" "Prego? Non ne ho idea! Scusami!" "Non c'e problema!"

"Grazie." "Arrivederci!" "Caio!"

There, we've exercised our brains for one day. We've got this, boomers.

June 30, 2011

Don't Forget My Senior Discount

"Only $4.68,' he said cheerfully. I stood there stupefied. I am 48, not even 50 yet—a mere child! Senior Citizen (discount)? I took my burrito and walked out to the truck wondering what was wrong."

—David McClure, *The Dallas Morning News* Community Opinion

The first time I was asked by a cashier if I wanted the "senior-coffee discount" I was indignant.

Now, I gladly pay half-price or less and smile back.

Since I first wrote awhile back about my chagrin and outright disdain at being asked if I wanted a senior discount, things have changed.

I signed up for early Social Security and now look forward to my instant direct deposit like the best of them.

I order senior portions at restaurants.

And yes, I now take the senior-coffee discount at McDonald's without complaint.

Let's just call it a rite of passage into the world of seniors. Now, I sort of like it.

The evolution and transformation in my thinking began when a young cashier, all of twelve in my humble view, charged me $0.27 for a cup of coffee rather than full price.

She didn't ask if I was a "senior"; she assumed.

"Twenty-seven cents?" I asked incredulously.

"Yes," she said. "I gave you the senior discount."

"And what age would that be," I replied sternly.

A look of horror swept over her face as she realized what she said and the grave sin she had committed.

All women know innately that to assume another woman's age is tantamount to, shall we say, murder?

This young thing was beginning to figure out that it is not a good idea to tell a woman she is your senior. It is just fine if she tells you, but not a good plan to mention that fact to her first.

I give the youngster some credit for figuring this out so quickly; however, she would not raise her head or look at me for the rest of the transaction. She just mumbled, "Well, you can get it at any age." Nice catch.

The first thing I did when I got in the car was to inspect my face carefully and critically in the car rearview mirror.

I should have looked in the mirror on the outside passenger side where a little sticker warns us that objects might appear differently than they really are.

That would have cushioned the blow somewhat.

No, I chose instead to look in the painfully honest, exactly like-it-is mirror inside the car in broad, unforgiving daylight.

Yes indeed, I believe I do qualify for the senior coffee discount after all.

But in this recession-stricken world in which we live, I'll take that $0.27 any old day over the full-price $0.99 cup of coffee.

In fact, I am so excited now about senior discounts that I searched online for senior-discount-related apparel. Found a tote bag for me and hat for the hubby that has emblazoned upon them the phrase: "Don't forget my senior discount."

We'll only wear these when we travel. Don't tell our kids!

September 30, 2010

Using Colorful Words and
Mixing up Others Can Be Hilarious

One of the peccadilloes of aging is that we begin to pepper our language with curious and colorful words; another is that we mix up our words and often get our "tang all tonguled-up."

The quiddity of this phenomenon is that the listener generally understands each word uttered or at least the gist of them, and comprehends the speaker's intention, even without knowing the word's exact meaning.

For example, the other night my husband yawned and said, "I have to go to bed before I get 'pumpkinized.'" Meaning, he was getting tired and needed to go to bed before he "turned into a pumpkin."

Although his colorful speech could be called an outré (unconventional or eccentric) remark, I still got it just fine.

Recently, on the morning *Fox and Friends* television show, Marie Osmond commented, "If life gives you lemonade, make lemons."[4] Of course, she meant to say that phrase the other way around, but I understood her just the same.

My cousin who is a septuagenarian (and that is an important factor later in this story) is apt to say, "The sky is ominous today and portends a burgeoning storm with susurrus winds."

Her vocabulary of uncommon words is truly astonishing. I never ask their meaning, but occasionally, I admit that I do indeed run for a dictionary when she speaks. Actually, I am envious of her ability to spout uncommon words with such fluidity and ease.

Another example: Last night on the television show *Boston Legal*, William Shatner's aging character pontificated that he could have a jury in the palm of his lap any time he wanted by using his gift of soaring and emotional rhetoric.

"Don't you mean to say 'hand'?"a young colleague snarked back.[5] Well, I understood Shatner, I thought, more than a little annoyed that the young guy had to correct him.

Thankfully, here is some good news, readers. There is a plausible explanation why, as we age, we mix up words and a very good reason why we may verbalize a rare word from time to time.

I can only say, "Thank goodness there is a reason!" Yet, I am tired of explaining why I say synonym when I mean to say that brown spicy substance you may know as cinnamon.

I spew out spoonerisms (words and phrases in which letters or syllables get swapped) with the best of them:

Go and shake a tower, when I mean, go take a shower.

You had better get movin' at the lead of spite, meaning at the speed of light.

That is a lack of pies if I ever heard one, meaning a pack of lies.

However, I did promise to explain why there is a good reason for colorful language misuse and why a septuagenarian (a seventy-something year old) is important to this story.

Dr. Gitit Kavé , a clinical neuro-psychologist from the Herczeg Institute of Aging, conducted a study on the effects of aging on language and says there is a significant decrease in word retrieval abilities after the age of seventy.

According to Dr. Kavé , "As we grow older, we acquire more words and our vocabulary grows . . . Paradoxically, the older you are, the richer your vocabulary and yet the harder it is for you to produce a specific word. But because older people's vocabulary is larger and they know many words that are rarely used, older people may use those rare ones instead of retrieving a more common word."

I don't know about that explanation. It really doesn't tease my ears. You knew I meant to say "ease my tears," didn't you?

Or, was it "ease my fears," I meant to say? I have no earthly idea.

April 23, 3009

20

Cleaning out the Basement Closet
is Scary but Illuminating

*"One of the advantages of being disorderly is that
one is constantly making exciting discoveries."*

—A.A. MILNE

As in my scary basement closet.

Perhaps it was the new moon this week that drew me to the large closet in our basement, urging me to clean it.

Perhaps it was that someone asked me to find something there.

My reply to that person, "You wonder if I have it. I wonder where it is. Everybody wonders how I find it."

At least twice a year I try.

Whether it was the drive of the new moon or a need to find something, I began to search the closet we call "the cave."

I braced myself for brave entry into this inner *sanctum sanctorum* deep within the bowels of this edifice of our home.

I told you it was a scary place.

When we originally built the house, we poured concrete walls and a concrete ceiling under the garage in the basement. The idea was to have a climate-controlled storage area and tornado shelter.

Now, that room is merely a disorganized and disorderly closet full of life memorabilia.

Taking a serious look at this most private and secret room bred the need to organize, discard, and donate. One cannot escape the powerful force calling one to sort, systematize, arrange, and classify when one finally tackles cleaning out the closet.

Mark Twain once said this about keeping things in closets: "Have a place for everything and keep the thing somewhere else; this is not a piece of advice, it is merely a custom."

Now, I see why climate-controlled storage lockers outside of one's home are the rage.

Keep all your saved things somewhere other than in your own closet and home. That way you can hang onto them to your heart's content without looking at the clutter and without venturing into scary basement closets.

Erma Bombeck, famed humorist and columnist of the '60s, had a theory on housework that applies just as well to cleaning out closets. Erma quipped, "My theory on housework is, if the item doesn't multiply, smell, catch fire, or block the refrigerator door, let it be. No one else cares. Why should you?"

On second thought, maybe twice a year is too often to visit our scary closet in the basement. I am checking out climate-controlled storage lockers as we speak.

October 30, 2008

To Stay Young, Learn Something New

"I grow old learning something new every day."
—**SOLON**, Athenian statesman and poet of 630–560 BC

The month of January is the perfect time to learn something new, the secret elixir that keeps us young; that is, according to the philosophy of my late Great-Aunt Ida. She died still perfectly lucid at the age of ninety-eight.

I often said of her that I wanted to grow up and be just like her. Not an easy task, I am discovering.

However, I am making a valiant effort by trying to learn something new each day just like she did. Since I do not have her penchant for remembering baseball statistics or her proclivity for geography, I have resolved to simply follow the news every day and pick up one new fact or learn one new truth.

Here is what I have learned so far in the month of January.

I have committed to memory the definition of Frisbeetarianism, a noun: the belief that, after death, the soul flies up onto the roof and gets stuck there. I found this new word in a *Washington Post* contest in which readers can submit new words or alternate meanings for common words. My second favorite was the word coffee. New meaning: the person upon whom one coughs.

An advertisement on television sells a video guide titled "How to use a metal detector," and I may have to order one yet this month. Certainly, that would qualify as a brand-new skill, and one I have never previously considered learning. I hear it is quite popular, too.

Also, I am learning more about the disclaimers on bottles of prescription medicines, especially when they warn, "How this medicine works is not completely understood." Yep, better learn more about that one if I want to emulate Aunt Ida's age.

23

Here is a new word I learned, and I am betting you do not know it either. Deipnosophist, a noun. It means someone who is skilled in table talk and is pronounced dyp-NOS-uh-fist. There you go, a brand-new fact. Now, I just have to master witty table talk.

TXT (text) messaging. This is a must-learn new skill, like it or not.

For instance, and I am speaking now to everyone over the age of forty who has not mastered TXT messaging, remember this new fact. When you go to the mall and you cannot read the warning signs because they are written in TXT messaging lingo, it is time to learn.

It took me awhile, but I have now mastered the mall warning sign aimed at those who tend to group and "hang out" at the mall. Wonder if this applies to the early morning mall walkers? Hmmm?

The sign reads: U Yell, U Cuss, U Group, U Gone.

Got it. Another skill learned.

NJOY and learn something new in January.

January 11, 2008

Winnie the Pooh Would Like a "No-Doing Day"

"Don't underestimate the value of doing nothing, of just going along, listening to all the things you can't hear, and not bothering."[6]

—**WINNIE THE POOH** to Piglet, *Pooh's Little Instruction Book*

The other day when I visited my ninety-one-year-old mother in the Alzheimer's special care facility in which she lives, I came away completely awestruck at the conversation I witnessed.

Let's call it a "teaching moment." Hopefully, I learned something, such as the fact that doing nothing can be a remarkable thing.

The discourse at the lunch table in the nursing home went like this.

I spoke first to a gentleman seated at Mom's table, "Hi Mr. Smith (we'll call him that), what are you doing today?"

"Nothing. What are you doing?" he replied.

I answered, leaving out the uninteresting details of my jammed-packed day ahead, "Well, nothing, I guess."

"That's what you should be doing—nothing," someone else added. "It's a No-Doing Day."

"Really," I said. "I could use a No-Doing Day. I like that! Let's start a club."

Another spoke up immediately and added, "Yes, and we will have no meetings."

Mr. Smith then sternly admonished me, "I don't expect you to show up."

My mother, in an unusual moment of clarity, joined in the conversation, turning to me, saying, "Kay Jean, you should take a nap."

So, upon that directive, we moved to the television room and settled in the recliners to watch *The Andy Griffith Show* and *Mayberry RFD*. We both nodded off.

As I was leaving the unit, actually refreshed no doubt from the nap I was ordered to take, one of the staffers winked and then whispered to me, "Yunno, I think Monday may just be a No-Doing Day for me." Reflecting on this interesting afternoon, I could not help but recall a childhood book and one of its many dialogues between Winnie the Pooh and his sidekick Christopher Robin.

Incidentally, if you want to brush up on Pooh philosophizing, I recommend the *The Complete Tales of Winnie the Pooh*, in which Pooh emerges as one of the best philosophers of all time. And dear readers, you might also enjoy a look at just-pooh.com where you will find a fascinating history of the "magical world of Pooh."

But as I was saying . . .

Winnie the Pooh asked Christopher Robin, "How do you do just nothing?"

Christopher Robin: "Well, when grown-ups ask, 'What are you going to do?' and you say, 'Nothing,' and then you go and do it."

Winnie the Pooh: "I like that. Let's do it all the time."

Well, maybe not all the time, but at least for one day, our very own "No-Doing Day."

And naps are good, too.

October 1, 2009

You Will Always Be You—What I Didn't Expect About Getting Older

*"If I knew I was going to live this long,
I would have taken better care of myself."*

—MICKEY MANTLE

At a relative's ninetieth birthday celebration, one guest asked the honoree, "Say, how does it feel to be ninety?"

"I don't know," came his quick retort. "I feel about the same way I always have. How old are you, thirty-five? So, how does it feel to be thirty-five?" Then, he winked and smiled.

Ah, what does it feel like indeed, I wondered?

I guess as we age, we expect to feel "old," but what I didn't expect about getting older is that we don't really feel that "old" in our heart of hearts. Our bodies may feel weaker, but in our souls, we are still sixteen or twenty-five or thirty-five.

We are the same people we always were. That surprises me.

I like what '90s journalist and essayist I.F. Stone said that surprised him about aging: "When you are younger you get blamed for crimes you never committed, and when you're older you begin to get credit for virtues you never possessed. It evens itself out."

And so it does.

I was pondering all these thoughts (not too seriously you understand, because keep in mind I still feel about sixteen) when into my email inbox pops my quarterly college alumni newsletter.

There, to my delight, were short essays from dear old friends giving updates about their lives, stories of family, career, and retirement. What caught my eye, however, was a universal underlying theme—aging isn't exactly what they expected.

I love my friend Connie's story she titled, "It's me."

Connie writes that she is still the same person she always was, something she did not expect at all about getting older.

Here are some excerpts: "Honestly, I expected much of what has happened in the intervening years (since college). Arthritis and gray hair, after all, are part of the old lady uniform. Right? What I didn't expect was that I would be pretty nearly the same person that I was."

She reminisces: "Back in the '60s, when I was a college student, we tended to view older people as significantly different from us. They just didn't 'get it.' We—or, at least, I—thought that people changed as they aged. They do change, but not in all the ways I feared. I'm still Connie.

"OK. I gained a lot of weight. My hair is white. I have had a knee replacement, so I wobble a little.

"I thought I would be cranky, judgmental, and anything but fun to be around when I got old. Not true! I whine a lot sometimes, but I'm not really cranky. And I've never been judgmental, so why would I start now?

"I'm the same inside! This is the big secret! You will always be you."

However, Connie and I agree that the above "secret of aging" should come with a disclaimer, a warning if you will.

Here it is: Yes, it's true you will always be you, but you will be an "old you" before you know what's happened!

"When I was young, I was called a rugged individualist. When I was in my fifties, I was considered eccentric. Here I am doing and saying the same things I did then, and now I'm labeled senile."[7]

—GEORGE BURNS in *Just You and Me, Kid*, 1979

September 1, 2011

Happy Boomer Days

"I'm not an empty nester. With my life coach, family advice, and psychologist I have no time for that!"

Boomers Won't Go Quietly

*"I'll bet when the Bee Gees sing 'Staying Alive' these days it takes
on a special poignancy with aging audiences. And isn't it time
that Jerry and the Pacemakers made a comeback?"*

—BILL GEIST

In the year ahead, both George W. Bush and Bill Clinton will turn
sixty.

Statisticians say there are 78 million baby boomers, born between
1946 and 1964.

AP national writer David Crary filed a story at the end of 2005 in
which he said of the baby boomer phenomenon:

"They partied and protested, then grew up to dominate America
with their chutzpah and sheer numbers. Yet now, as the oldest of
the baby boomers prepare to turn sixty, there are glimmers of doubt
within this 'have it all' generation about how they will be judged by
those who come next."[8]

Crary does concede that Ron Kovic, author of *Born on the Fourth
of July*, begs to differ.

I have to agree with Mr. Kovic on some of his points; namely,
when he says that boomers are just as strong as they ever were.

Kovic says, "We have every reason to be proud. We were brash
and bold and beautiful . . . Often when people get older, they say to
the younger generation, 'Well, it's your turn now.' I feel very differently. Rather than just passing the torch, and saying we did our best,
this generation, which dreamed such big, impossible dreams, refuses
to step aside. It sees itself as part of change that it still passionately
believes will occur."[9]

Amen.

Boomers, we do not need a comeback. We never left.

31

Either way you look at it, baby boomers have put a decidedly different slant on this aging business than have previous generations.

Furthermore, most of us boomers do not really care what history writes of us or how future generations judge us.

Never has a generation before or since experienced such an unbridled run of success.

It has not gone to our heads either.

Boomers seem to know, innately, that we would be everlastingly wrong if we were to assume that what we think and feel only affects us.

We know all things are universal.

Truth is, boomers sense that everyone feels pretty much the same way, have the same doubts and fears, suffer hardships, learn to rise above them, and marvel at the surprise of grace, joy, and forgiveness when it appears.

Boomers, no stranger to adversity, may have scars, but nearly all come out stronger, or die trying.

Throw us all into a sack, and we come out pretty much the same. No exceptions.

Therein, lies the strength and the longevity of the baby boomer generation—a collective understanding of "team spirit."

And one more thing must be said of boomers: They are, simply put, very interesting folks.

Actress Katharine Hepburn once observed, "I have no romantic feelings about age. Either you are interesting at any age or you are not."

Few would argue that baby boomers are not interesting! They always have been.

Today, that lively and fascinating '60s generation is ready and able to tackle the '60s one more time.

Once again, they will do it with all the gusto and moxie they have exhibited since the day they were born.

For all those boomers turning sixty this year and for those soon to follow suit, a celebration is in order.

Throw a party and dance until dawn.

On second thought, maybe a movie and popcorn would do just fine. Nah, I am planning a party!

January 14, 2006

A Beatles Song Triggers Memories

"I Want to Hold Your Hand" was playing in the background at a favorite college hangout when a young woman asked me a question that gave me pause.

Brianna asked incredulously, "Did girls really swoon over the Beatles back in the '60s?"

So, what would any self-respecting Beatles fan do but sing a few lines from the song.

To my surprise, some of the college kids knew a few words from that Beatles' classic and joined in the chorus.

I return to Brianna's question: Did girls really faint, "fall over dead," black out, lose consciousness, collapse when the Beatles appeared on stage or television?

My answer—of course, they did. I was one of them.

Well, OK, I did not exactly faint—maybe, just drooped a bit.

Come February 9, 1964, though, I was parked "front and center" and as close as I could get to our state-of-the-art, black and white RCA box television.

A room full of high school friends, mostly girls, waited with me, frenzied with excitement.

Amused eyewitnesses said later that, indeed, we were hysterical.

Girls were shaking, some were short of breath, and their hearts were racing.

Most of the boys in the room were frowning, and my dad, watching from the dining room, thought we were all out of our minds.

He had only recently come to grips with the likes of Elvis's gyrating hips.

Now, the Beatles were invading America.

Reluctantly, my dad watched this horde of silly girls shriek and swoon over those long-haired, skinny English boys who sported outrageous, identical haircuts and matching black suits.

Not a pretty sight. The girls, I mean.

Through my frenzied stupor, I do seem to recall that my dad was chuckling quite a bit at the sight of us, despite his obvious displeasure.

Even though my dad humored us, the Beatles were not popular in some circles.

A few folks thought the Beatles personified the devil himself, just as they had when Elvis sang his way to fame in the '50s with "Blue Suede Shoes." A small amount of radio disc jockeys refused to play any music from England, saying they only gave airtime to American artists. Some of those very same American recording artists did not like the Beatles either. Even Frank Sinatra was not impressed with the Beatles' music, saying it was crude and that they were not very good musicians.

The naysayers were no match, though, for the throngs of teenage girls, and eventually guys, who joined in the adoration.

When Ed Sullivan introduced the Beatles on that special night in February, the cameras panned the crowd, showing girl after girl keeling over backwards into the pack.

No one, dear college friends, is making any of this up.

As America watched, through the miracle of television, viewers agreed that never had there been such a phenomenon as those worshipful Beatles fans.

The fans were as much a part of this rare spectacle as the Beatles themselves.

In fact, just days before *The Ed Sullivan Show*, the Beatles had been met at the JFK Airport in New York by a massive crowd of devotees. The Beatles' arrival at the airport caused near chaos and was the beginning of "Beatlemania" in the United States.

Approximately 40 percent of the US population at the time, 73 million people, watched in awe when the Beatles performed their magic on *The Ed Sullivan Show*. Today, those numbers remain as one of the largest viewing audiences ever recorded in the history of the country.

The Beatles were so popular that Ed Sullivan had them back two more times in February of 1964 on his "really big shew!"

Three weeks of this mania just about drove my dad and many other parents to the end of what little patience they had left.

They had no idea, however, that we were only just beginning our obsession with the Beatles.

It was not long after that, my sister Pat, two friends, Sue and Priscilla, and I thought it would be great fun to impersonate the Beatles at school talent performances and dances. We found Beatles wigs, wore black suits, and lip-synched their songs, long before most anyone had ever even used the term "lip-synching."

I cannot imagine what my dad must have thought, but he never reprimanded us once. He was probably having too much fun laughing. In no time at all, the entire world, not just our little corner, was won over by the Beatles. Their army of silly girl fans soon gave way to legions of devoted followers.

To my young college friends, I must add this very important fact—Beatles lyrics never leave the soul of a true Beatles fan. The Beatles sang "Love me do."

And, we still do.

February 25, 2006

The Commencement Speech
I Can't Remember

*"It ain't what you don't know that gets you into trouble.
It's what you know for sure that just ain't so."*

—MARK TWAIN

It is graduation time, and therefore, inspirational speeches about how to live one's life are profluent. I am feeling nostalgic about mine.

From Dr. Seuss to Steve Jobs, there is plenty of advice to be absorbed at commencements.

Great speeches, great quotes, great words by which to guide a young graduate's life.

But do we pay attention to the speaker? I wish I had.

I am certain that our high school commencement address was inspirational, if not prophetic, but I didn't hear a word.

I would settle for recalling the title of our commencement address back in 1965, but alas, I cannot remember much about that evening.

Well yes, there is one thing—my shoe. You see, I was consumed with looking for my suddenly missing brand new, white high heel pump, not with listening to the speaker.

Here's what happened.

The new shoe rubbed my foot so badly that I slipped it off during the speaker's address. Voila! Just like that it disappeared and stayed gone throughout the senior class president's speech, the announcement of our class flower and colors, and through special numbers by the junior class girls' vocal group and our award-winning high school trumpet trio.

I panicked, but continued to smile and to keep a brave face on despite my outright terror at the idea of walking across the stage with only one high heel shoe and having to hobble lopsided.

I whispered, begging to my neighbors on stage, "Please, find my left high heel pump. Hurry."

It was going to be my turn soon to walk across the stage and shake hands with our superintendent who would not think it funny at all that I had only one shoe.

Additionally, there would be my mother to contend with later, and I didn't even want to entertain that thought.

What should I do? Kick off the other shoe and walk barefoot across the stage? It was 1965 and we didn't do such things then. That didn't start happening until the '90s, did it?

I pleaded with my friends in the back row, but they thought the whole thing hilarious and believed that I probably had it coming anyway.

The sneaky complicit ones in the back row watched this spectacle play out, delighting in the fact that the shoe bandit was slick. No one in the audience saw the heist, or so they later said. The senior girls remained mum, while some senior boys, Robert, Steve, Harvey, and Stephen in particular, pretended they knew the identity of the culprit.

One of them told me it was Hugh.

Hugh shook his head no, but he did produce the shoe and pass it down the aisle just in time for me to walk across the stage to receive my diploma. I laughed, my friends laughed, and everyone thought it was great fun.

The shoe caper was history, I thought.

Epilogue: Last year I attended my forty-fifth high school class reunion. Sitting across the banquet table from me was a classmate I hadn't seen in years. He said hello and grinned, chuckling to himself, "You don't recognize me, do you? I'm Hugh."

"Hugh," I said. "Hugh of the graduation shoe caper that almost got me in big trouble?"

"What do you mean?" he said. "I didn't take your shoe. I'm the one who got it back for you in the nick of time. I saved the day."

"Steve told me you took it," I said incredulously.

"Do you mean that for forty-five years you blamed me for taking your shoe when it was probably Steve all along?" Hugh laughed.

"By the way," he continued, "Do you happen to remember the name of our commencement speaker and what he said? I can't remember a thing. I was too busy trying to rescue your shoe."

May 19, 2011

College Move-in Day Tough on Parents

In the month of August of every year, college-bound students pack their myriad of belongings and leave home.

For the freshman, it is often their first time away. You can spot them easily that initial day on campus.

They are the ones who flee as far away as possible from their embarrassing baby boomer parents.

For others, upper classman or career students, college move-in day is "old hat."

Mom and Dad do not mortify them quite so much anymore.

Sophomores to seniors know that parents are good for a few necessities, notably food, cash, and gasoline for starters. It takes the frosh a bit longer to figure this out.

Upperclassmen actually enjoy their parents more than they did when they were freshmen. We cannot assume, however, that means parents are to stay any longer on move-in day than to unload, fix things, and provide food.

Upperclassmen are ready to be taken out to lunch immediately after they dump their possessions on the floor of their rooms.

Cash is the priority now. Skip the décor. Freshmen just want their parents to leave.

That fact, however, does not mean that all parents will leave. Some have been known to stay in a motel for a couple of weeks just to make sure their students are adjusting well and that all needs are met.

As a veteran of I-don't-know-how-many college move-in days, I do not recommend that parents hang around long.

It could get weird.

Whatever you do, if you are the parent of a fraternity guy, do not go upstairs in any fraternity house until Family Weekend!

After the freshman year has passed, parents of a sophomore may notice that their student does not need to spruce the new place up much. No one appears to care any longer if the bedspreads match or if there is a comfy rug on the floor.

Designer room décor will come back into the picture later when students move into apartments during their junior and senior years and beyond. Be ready then to visit a lot of furniture stores or garage sales.

And, as the unlucky of us know, some students do stay on into the "beyond" years.

One thing we parents learn through "the school of hard knocks" is that college move-in day is both physically and emotionally exhausting.

It does not matter if it is the first year or the fifth or even the eighth for some.

Oh, my.

By the way, I do not believe any parent who tells me they enjoy driving for hours to the chosen college in an overstuffed car full of boxes, shoes, and cleaning supplies.

Neither do parents thrill at the idea of pulling a U-Haul trailer crammed full of their student's belongings, only to have to unload in the rain and lug small refrigerators and microwaves to the third floor. Whenever other students appear on the scene, be warned. Parents will be shunned from that moment on and become invisible to their student, but not unnecessary.

Dads can be seen on college move-in day carrying their DeWalt power tool cases into the dorm rooms while moms are making at least three Walmart runs for more extension cords and curtain rods.

Why do parents gladly put themselves into servant mode year after year on college move-in days?

I am guessing it is because we are completely lost in this strange new way of life.

Simply put, we are lost at the prospect of living without our kids.

One way for parents to hold it together for a little while is to clean a room, drill holes, install closet organizers, and assemble a bed frame.

It helps.

Kids, on the other hand, are not sad at all. They are living in a room the size of most closets and lovin' it.

Parents find themselves alone for the first time without kids to supervise and with absolutely no idea how to refocus.

This new stage of life takes a bit longer for parents to love than it does for the college gang, say maybe two weeks. By then, we are dusting off our dreams and getting busy reinventing ourselves.

On move-in day there are a few perks worth noting.

Parents can commiserate with one another, comparing horror stories about college move-in days.

Students can commiserate with each other, comparing whose parents were the "nerdiest" and whose acted the most stupidly.

And years later, when no longer at odds, parents and grown kids finally get on the same page.

Once again, parents work hard to set up a new apartment for the recent college grad or help the newlyweds find their first house or paint a nursery.

Move-in days never end.

You will never want to be without them.

August 26, 2006

Empty Nest Syndrome
Isn't Always Depressing

Psychologists create new conditions with aplomb, and a faddy one of late is "empty nest syndrome."

Since baby boomers are now of the age when their offspring have flown the nest, and since there are so many of us in that category, "empty nest" seems to fit at first blush.

Life coaches, psychologists, and family experts are only doing their job when they counsel folks about the sadness and loss they experience when their kiddos leave home.

Do not get me wrong. I am sure there are some parents suffering mightily from this syndrome.

However, I have to wonder, where are they?

How many depressed "empty nesters" could there be anyway? No one I know.

My observation of "empty nesters" is quite different than that of the experts who apparently see boatloads of depressed parents who wander around aimlessly for weeks crying buckets of tears when their teens leave home.

I remember a cartoon I saw when my youngest child started school. I laughed out loud at the time. It applies now just the same as it did then. The cartoon strip followed a mom as she walked the last of her five children to the bus on her son's first day of kindergarten. She was telling him how much she would miss him but encouraged him to enjoy his first day of school.

As soon as the bus was out of sight, the mom in the cartoon pumped her fist into the air and yelled, "Yes!"

My thinking is there could be a lot of parents of college students saying "Yes," too.

My friend Cassie recently packed up and launched the last of her three children to a college miles away.

Cassie explained how she felt this way: "A milestone occurred in my life last week. David and I became empty-nesters when Link left for college.

"So, you may wonder, was it a sad event?

"Actually, I was kind of busy, so I didn't really notice.

"The same day that Link moved into the dorm, my dog, Roxy, and I had our first agility trial. I had been anticipating this competition for months, so launching the last-born just had to go on without me.

"Mind you, I didn't send my baby to parts unknown all by himself. Big sister, Becky, went along to help with the actual moving in. Link said that was much better anyway because she can carry a lot more stuff in one trip than I can.

"It's very exhilarating to have kids who are independent.

"I'm entering a new phase of my life, and I'm jumping in with both feet.

"My plans are to challenge myself in new ways and enjoy every day with enthusiasm and gratitude."

Thank you, Cassie. Words of wisdom indeed.

Lots of us are allowing ourselves the freedom to do the same and to enjoy our long-lost passions.

I, for one, have taken up writing again, and there are not enough hours in the day to accommodate this new-found pursuit.

Some couples delight in taking cruises to just about everywhere the cruise liners allow.

Some take extended weekends to the lake.

Others take up long-lost hobbies such as fishing or restoring old tractors.

Dennis, a widower, is off to DC whenever he can to spend days visiting the endless array of museums there.

Jim took a different job, something brand new that challenges his creativity and allows him to travel.

Margaret is quilting once again after years of neglecting her much-loved hobby.

As Cassie says, "I hope that you will also nurture the joyful you and allow yourself the freedom to enjoy your passions. Then, when life makes an adjustment—like when all of your children grow up and leave home—you won't find yourself floundering for fulfillment."

One of Cassie's favorite sayings goes like this, "Wherever you go, there you are."

May you find yourself in good company.

September 9, 2006

The Dawn of a New Error

I saw the quote "Every morning is the dawn of a new error" on a tee shirt somewhere, but I can't remember where or I would go back and buy one. Truth is, I can't remember a lot these days.

It wasn't always like that.

When I was twenty-one and living in my first apartment, the insurance agent said I needed to catalogue each item in every drawer and closet in case of loss or damage. I told him "no," that would not be necessary since I could sit down right now and provide him with a list of every single belonging.

I had a great memory then and not much stuff. Today, I have a lot of stuff and not much memory.

I am sorry to say that life for those of a certain age is becoming what Sharon told me the other day on the phone, or was it Susan? I think it was Sharon.

"At our age, we are in lower gear but still propelling forward, and our ship is sinking just like our memory."

"Oh, that is profound," I said. "I have to write that down. I will never remember it."

She called me back five minutes later and said. "Do you happen to remember what I just told you? I can't. I hope you wrote it down because I want to remember it, too."

At least I am not in the boat alone.

The next day, I was on a short road trip with Susan (I am certain it was Susan), and as we drove along, we lamented our loss of memory. She told me about a new book just published about forgetting everything and about growing old.

Intrigued, I asked Susan, "What's the name of the book?"

Susan said, "I can't remember a thing."

"Me either," I replied and laughed. Exasperated, she tried again.

"*I Can't Remember a Thing*," she reiterated, meaning that was the name of the book.

I still didn't get it, and from there our conversation became a remake of Abbott and Costello's famed "Who's on First" sketch.

Turns out, the book to which Susan was referring was actually Nora Ephron's novel, *I Remember Nothing*. I learned the correct title from my friend, Beth.

Giggle, giggle—I got the last laugh after all because Susan didn't remember the name of the book correctly.

That scenario happened last week, most of which as you can tell, I have since forgotten. Now, I find myself wondering if it was in fact Susan who told me about the title of the book first and Beth second, or vice versa.

Never mind; it doesn't matter. I located the correct title. I simply Googled it.

Its author Nora Ephron, famed novelist and screenwriter, "googles" a lot, too.

In fact, she says that we are living in the Google years, and for those of us who can remember nothing, that is a good thing.

Nora writes: "When you forget something, you can whip out your iPhone and go to Google. The Senior Moment has become the Google Moment, and it has a much nicer, hipper, younger, more contemporary sound, doesn't it."

She explains more: "By handling the obligations of the search mechanism you almost prove you can keep up . . . There's none of the nightmare of the true Senior Moment—the long search for the answer . . . you just go to Google and retrieve it.

"You can't retrieve your life (unless you're on Wikipedia, in which case you can retrieve an inaccurate version of it). But you can retrieve the name of that actor who was in that movie, the one about World War II . . . or the name of that song that was sung by that singer, the one about love. You know the one."

But sometimes, she says, "I'm forced to conclude that I remember nothing."[10]

Me, too, because I just misplaced my iPhone and, for the moment, cannot Google. I think Sharon (or was it Susan or was it Beth?) was right. My ship is indeed sinking.

February 10, 2011

Boomers Can Do Math
without Calculators

The memory of baby boomers may be the only thing that saves the lost art of manually finding a square root. Some of us remember how. Some of us could care less. I am in the latter group.

Regardless of whether you like math or not, baby boomers remember how to do it.

You may remember more about eighth grade math than you think, and you can probably do it without a calculator. You can figure percentage, solve long division problems, and know what a remainder is. You can recite quite a few multiplication tables, recall a little something about "casting out nines," and know pi (3.14), the number that goes on forever.

Ask your kids and grandkids to sit down with a piece of paper and pencil and try and to solve a square root or even a long division problem without their calculators. Well, let us just say I am betting on you. Do not get me wrong, I am not waxing poetic or becoming romantic about numbers, although many folks do. Granted, there is a certain beauty in numbers.

However, as I recall from my college days, budding journalists like myself were notorious for disliking math and avoiding it at all costs. Therefore, it did my heart good recently to hear a college dean mention that journalism students have not changed much. Apparently, they still function best on the language side of their brains where no math problems abide nor are wanted by we writer types.

I must confess, though, that I can actually remember an eighth-grade math definition of "square root," which is this: "The square root of a number is another number that when multiplied by itself gives you the first number."

Do not get too impressed here because I am merely talking about finding the square root of a simple number such as sixteen. That is easy enough; the answer is four because four times itself gives you the first number, sixteen. One can do this with any number one wants, but I hate to tell you the bad news—only a few numbers like sixteen work out so nicely. To find the square root of most numbers, one can keep the decimal places going for as long as one likes, but I cannot imagine why one would want to do that.

There are those among us, though, who love math so much that they celebrate math holidays such as March 14, also known to pi lovers as 3.14. Get it?

That is over the top for me as I still have horrific memories of eighth-grade math word problems.

By the time I finished reading those long word problems back then, I was positively worn out and ready for PE over pi any day.

You remember those tricky problems of which I speak.

A passenger train leaves the Philadelphia train depot two hours after a freight train from Boston leaves the same depot. The freight train is traveling 20 mph slower than the passenger train. Find the rate of each train, if the passenger train overtakes the freight train in three hours.

No!

My brain does not work this way.

Eventually, I learned that where the freight train originally came from had absolutely nothing to do with solving the problem.

I am afraid I am like the chef who said to his helper, "You take two-thirds of water, one-third of cream, one-third of broth . . . "

The apprentice replied, "But that makes four-thirds already!"

"Well," said the chef, "just get a bigger pot!"

Makes perfect sense to me. Who needs a calculator?

March 24, 2007

When a Computer Dies, Grief Sets In

"I do not fear computers. I fear the lack of them."
—Isaac Asimov, US science fiction novelist
and scholar, 1920–1992

When one's home computer is down, communication halts and frustration mounts. The entire experience is grief-like as we go through the stages of shock, denial, anger, and resignation.

When my computer died, I gave up and cleaned the house.

So, I am compelled to share with you this philosophical question I read recently: Does a clean house indicate there is a broken computer in it?

It took a broken computer to get my house clean. Perhaps, the garage will be my next project, and then, and most unbelievably, putting photos in scrapbooks.

Does anyone really do that?

But I digress. At first, when this catastrophic event happened, that is the computer's untimely demise, I ran around in a tizzy trying to get it fixed. Eventually after much weeping and wailing and gnashing of teeth, I realized that the ditch was the best place for the contraption.

I like what Joe Martin, cartoonist for *Porterfield*, said about computers, "The most overlooked advantage to owning a computer is that if they foul up there's no law against whacking them around a bit." Generally speaking, we are far better off to buy a new computer and start all over rather than punch the old one. However, a new computer means we will need a new printer and new software so that all components are compatible.

I know you have seen this movie, and it is always expensive.

So, with the computer temporarily out of commission, I rediscovered my neighbors and finished my Christmas thank you notes.

Soon, I plan to tackle spring housecleaning, wash windows, and work on taxes.

Someone please come and save me, not from the neighbors you understand, just the window washing and the taxes!

All this productive activity was becoming a dangerous situation, indeed, so there was nothing left to do but take a computer class. For you fellow computer junkies, well, what can I say other than it is pure heaven.

Now, all I need besides the basics of a new computer, service plan, and more lessons, is more memory. For we baby boomers, more memory might be first on our list.

There is only one other thing I should mention about computers and our love for them.

When your significant other is a computer, you could be a tad over the top.

Or, maybe not.

January 25, 2008

Does Anyone Eat
Liver and Onions Anymore?

"As a child, my family's menu consisted of two choices: take it or leave it."
—Buddy Hackett

The other day I watched someone order liver and onions in a restaurant, and instantly I remembered why I hated it as a child.

It was the smell.

No, on second thought, it was the taste. In fact, I still remember what it tastes like some fifty years later—shoe leather with a pungent, strong flavor that makes chicken gizzards seem like child's play.

Thus, I have to ask, "Does anyone eat liver and onions anymore?" No, do not answer; just cut me some slack as I explain.

Liver and onions, as baby boomers recall, was a required monthly staple in most households. We ate it, or were forced to eat it for its iron. If one felt anemic or weak, Grandma said to eat liver.

However, eating this natural iron supplement also involves the inescapable idea of consuming an organ that has the primary responsibility of filtering out the body's impurities. Shudder.

Now, I will hear from people.

There is one more thing I should mention about liver. In elementary schools in the '50s and '60s, it was not uncommon for teachers to make children sit for hours in the lunchroom until they choked down the liver.

Can you imagine that today? Everyone would be on the six o'clock news.

But I digress; consider the case of sweet Cindy B. versus the teacher who made her sit until 2:00 p.m. until she ate every bite of her liver and onions. Cindy was a bit shy and could only sit and cry as she shook her pretty head "no" at the teacher.

Finally, one day after this continued far too long, my sister felt sorry for her and said, "Cindy, next time here is what you do. Drink your milk, cut the liver into tiny pieces, pretend to eat it, and when the teacher isn't looking stuff the liver in your milk carton."

My sister joked that she could have a life of crime in her future for even thinking up such a scheme as a second-grader.

I said no; I thought the plan brilliant.

However, dear reader, if you absolutely insist on reverting to our grandparents' day to replicate a family-favorite liver dish, I will offer the following recipe from memory.

Coat the calves' liver in flour, sprinkle liberally with salt and pepper, and fry (in a cast iron skillet) with sliced onions until golden brown in bacon fat or butter.

One can soak the liver in milk to eliminate the funky taste, drown it in catsup, coat it in crumbs and chicken-fry it, or cover it with gravy.

Or not.

April 11, 2008

Middle Years Bring Embarrassing Changes

"In a man's middle years there is scarcely a part of the body he would hesitate to turn over to the proper authorities."[11]

—E.B. White

In our middle years we realize, often by happenstance, that strange things are occurring in our bodies. Most of us do not like it one bit either.

But as my grandmother used to say, "What's a body to do?" I say scream and knock one's head against the nearest wall.

Granted that will not solve the problem, but consider our quite justified lamentations about middle age and our changing bodies.

We now have unwanted hair in places we never had it before, and we have no hair or thinning hair in places where it used to be abundant. We have creaking, painful, stiff knees that not too long ago could run a 5K or could fly up the stairs in a single bound. We were Superman and Superwoman!

Nowhere in our previously nicely appointed and un-hospital like boudoirs would we find the following: Bengay for painful joints, nose spray for stuffed sinuses, eye drops for dry eyes, tissues, drinking water for cotton mouth during the night, reading glasses, knee bolsters, neck rests, and shoe inserts for plantar fasciitis.

Once one turns fifty, trust me, these items begin to appear in one's bedroom.

It is not a pretty sight.

Did I mention vitamins and pills? I didn't think so, as I am trying to forget that dreary fact. After arriving at age fifty, taking pills for multiple reasons becomes an undeniable part of daily life.

I like poet James Doyle's view of this as he takes a funny poke at pill-taking in an online-published poem for seniors titled "Vitamins."

Doyle pretends to be hunting for a pill-taking mate in the newspaper personals. He writes, "If there are others out there / who also take twenty-three / pills at a time four times / every day, please contact me / through the personals. We can / help each other force them down."

He continues, "Time release / capsules for dry bone, bleached / desert rats gulping down canteen / after canteen. What couple could / have more in common than a continual / dissolving? I am a young seventy-nine. / Looking for a minimum taker of sixty / pills daily. Call me if you want / to twist some tops off. Lets rattle / the bottle till they're gone. Smokers okay."[12]

I think it is time for my nap.

September 25, 2008

Boomer Forgetfulness
Makes Song a Hit Video

---

*"Looking for my wallet and car keys, well they can't have gone too far.
Just as soon as I find my glasses, I'm sure I'll see just where they are."*[13]

—TOM RUSH, folk and blues singer-songwriter

From time to time in this "Full Circle" column, I try to bring my generation up to speed on the latest trends and fads that affect us. I love to surf the web. It is my thing, but it may not be yours, and that is perfectly okay.

This time, however, many of you are well ahead of me. Millions of us have already clicked on YouTube to watch a musical video by Tom Rush, folksy guitarist and singer-songwriter of the '60s. His big YouTube hit is titled "Looking for my wallet and my car keys," but it is commonly known as "The Remember Song."

Tom says this on his website about his YouTube phenomenon, "I have been waiting forty-five years to become an overnight sensation, and it's finally happened!"

He continues, "My 'Remember Song' is up over 3.5 million plays and counting. What's interesting to me is that clearly these are not three million kids watching this thing—it's the boomers, who are supposed to be Luddites (term used to describe anyone opposed to technological change and progress) but apparently aren't!"

YouTube, for non-computer users, is a video sharing website where users can upload short video movies.

Trust me, I do not explain YouTube to you with any condescension or superciliousness in mind at all. Rather, it is because I am well aware that there are many of us boomers who could be called "e-challenged"—my husband, my cousin, my neighbor for starters.

And, it is just fine, and do not let anyone say otherwise. I might have to slap them around a bit if they do.

But back to Tom Rush.

He comments on his website about this hot YouTube song, "A video clip of my performance of 'The Remember Song' has gone viral. I felt terrible at first thinking I was being accused of being a musical equivalent of Ebola (common term for a group of viruses), but my children explained to me that this was a good thing."

Take a listen to one more verse.

"Supposed to meet someone for lunch today, but I can't remember where. Or who it is I am meeting. It is in my organizer somewhere. I might've left it on the counter. Maybe outside in the car. The last time I remember driving was to that memory enhancement seminar."[14]

Lost wallet, car keys, organizers. Drat. We can find YouTube though.

Right on, boomers.

September 18, 2008

Do You Have a Bucket List?

*"Life moves pretty fast. If you don't stop to
look around once in a while, you could miss it."*[15]

—FERRIS BUELLER (MATTHEW BRODERICK)
in *Ferris Bueller's Day Off,* 1986

Lately, I hear a lot about "bucket lists." People ask me, "Do you have one? Better make a bucket list if you don't. What is on your bucket list?"

I don't have one.

Occasionally, I would wonder what the term bucket list meant, but until recently I really did not have the time or inclination to find out.

I suppose I could if I were to watch the 2007 movie, *The Bucket List*, starring Jack Nicholson and Morgan Freeman. Apparently, it was a big box office success.

I didn't see it.

However, I surmise that the plot is about two terminally ill men who take a road trip to experience a wish list of things they want to do before they "kick the bucket."

Their bucket list was elaborate and daring, such as going skydiving, driving a motorcycle on the Great Wall of China, and attending a lion safari in Africa. Also on their list were more consequential items such as help a stranger for the simple and pure good of it and witness something truly majestic. I like the latter two best, as I am not too keen on performing motorcycle tricks on a wall.

As I explored the concept of a bucket list, I found several books with suggestions, but honestly most of the items I can skip without an ounce of regret.

I set out to make one of my own as I became increasingly intrigued by the idea. The project is going slowly, however, because I find reasons that make my choices impossible to accomplish.

Here is what I have so far:

- Take a month-long trip to Italy with my college girlfriends. (Not likely to happen unless one of us wins the lottery.)
- Write the book I always wanted to write and see it displayed in airport bookstores. It will be a story set in Italy during World War II, an unrequited love story. I envision it to be a cross between *The Bridges of Madison County* and *Saving Private Ryan*. (But I need an agent to make it a best seller and a trip to Italy to make it truly authentic. And of course, I need to write it.)
- Learn to speak Italian.

Apparently, there is a pattern here, something to do with Italy, I suppose.

What a feeble attempt, if I do say so myself.

Perhaps, I need to take some time this coming week to make a proper list. I am open to suggestions, dear readers, especially if you can figure out how I can spend a month in Italy.

We get busy and fall behind, far behind, on our daily tasks, don't we? In fact, I have a wooden plaque in my kitchen depicting a little turtle saying, "I'm so far behind I think I'm first."

And besides, who has time to make a bucket list?

Still, Dr. Seuss could be right when he asked, "What are we waiting for? Waiting for the fish to bite or waiting for wind to fly a kite. Or waiting around for Friday night or waiting perhaps for their Uncle Jake or a pot to boil or a better break or a string of pearls or a pair of pants or a wig with curls or another chance. Everyone is just waiting."[16] What is on your bucket list?

February 24, 2011

Patriotism
and
Politics

Puzzled by politics, perturbed by pundits,
and perplexed by pontificators.

On Independence Day, Whistle "Yankee Doodle" with the Fervor of John Adams

---

"Yankee Doodle went to town a-riding on a pony.
Stuck a feather in his cap and called it macaroni."

—Revolutionary War ditty

As we celebrate the Fourth of July this weekend, perhaps whistling the song "Yankee Doodle" is just what we need to do as we reflect on the birth of our nation, 233 years ago in 1776.

We must never forget that day and why it is important, either. Whistling and singing "Yankee Doodle" might help us do just that, if we do it with the gusto John Adams professed.

As I researched the history of July 4 to rejuvenate my memory, I remembered that July 2, not July 4, was the official date when the Second Continental Congress voted in a closed session to separate the American colonies from Great Britain. But the date July 4 is the date shown on the Declaration of Independence document, the date when the colonial government announced its independence to the world.

The exact date does not really matter anyway, as John Adams wrote in his now-famous note to his wife at the end of the colonists' world-changing congress. What does matter is how we remember and celebrate our nation's birth.

John Adams penned: "The second day (later celebrated as the fourth) of July, 1776, will be the most memorable epoch in the history of America. I am apt to believe that it will be celebrated by succeeding generations as the great anniversary festival. It ought to be commemorated at the day of deliverance by solemn acts of devotion to God Almighty. It ought to be solemnized with pomp and parade, with shows, games, sports, guns, bells, bonfires, and illuminations from one end of this continent to the other, from this time forward forever more."

I like what John Adams had to say.

In fact, I wish patriotism would come back in style with the fervor John Adams describes.

I wish we could unabashedly sing Yankee Doodle Dandy's light-hearted and whimsical tune without a cynic raising an annoyed eyebrow.

I wish folks would stick a small American flag in a flowerpot with pride, display an official flag with dignity and respect, and never, ever belittle it.

I wish the citizens of this great country would feel proud, very proud, of their fine country, the best experiment in freedom ever envisioned. I wish we would never hang our heads about the United States of America. I wish.

I wish when fireworks explode over ballparks and city parks this Fourth of July, that we collectively get a lump in our throats, that we swell with pride as the national anthem is sung.

I wish we would do all these patriotic things again without apology as we did in days and years gone by.

And yes, I wish folks would walk around whistling the light-hearted and whimsical Yankee Doodle Dandy refrain. It would bring a smile to my face. It would make you feel good, even if you are dressed up, as my cousin Al used to say.

Hey, Kermit the Frog sang "Yankee Doodle" and so did Barney and Friends. Caroline Kennedy named her pony "Macaroni," and it is the official State Song of Connecticut.

How can you go wrong with that? It won't hurt you, it will help you. So, won't you join me this Fourth of July by taking John Adams' words to heart and singing happily and proudly: "Father and I went down to camp, along with Captain Gooding. And there were all the men and boys as thick as hasty pudding. There was Captain Washington upon a slapping stallion; a giving orders to his men, I guess there was a million.

Yankee Doodle went to town a-riding on a pony. Stuck a feather in his cap and called it macaroni. Yankee Doodle, keep it up, Yankee Doodle Dandy. Mind the music and the step, and with the girls be handy."

Happy Fourth of July!

July 2, 2009

Straddling the Fence
is Not a Good Place to Be

Are you one of the undecideds in the middle this election year, a fence straddler? I hope not.

My dad often said that the middle of a fence was not a good place to be. He had a saying about fence straddlers. "That fellow spends so much time straddling that fence I am surprised he doesn't have splinters by now."

Who are you fence straddlers anyway? I want to meet you. I really want to meet you.

Where do you live? How do you think? An inquiring mind, mine, wants to know.

Can you really and truly not make up your mind yet about the election of 2008?

We are told almost daily by pundits that there are a vast number of undecideds who live somewhere in this country. We do not know exactly where they live, however.

We do not know who these uncommitted are, yet the political experts continue to tell us that these "Malcolms in the Middle" will decide the election.

I just want to meet one. A living, breathing human being who truly does not know what he or she wants yet.

Do these folks answer a poll question one way today and another way tomorrow based on the latest stump speech? Do they have a moveable sign in their yard that is easily changed as one vacillates between candidates?

Do they decide whom to support this week based solely on the latest television ad happily singing, "Oh, if I only had a brain?"

Does a candidate's slip of the tongue, a wrong word choice, a gaffe, a wink, or a hand gesture actually change a mind?

I am not buying any of this. How about you? We are smarter than that, are we not?

Think about this. Consider these numbers:

Forty percent of the country wants socialism and big government control, we are told; and forty percent want a capitalistic free market society.

Twenty percent are fuzzy and confused in the middle.

Thirty percent of Americans call themselves liberal and thirty percent call themselves conservative, ten percent call themselves very liberal and are part of the "blame and hate America first" crowd, and ten percent call themselves very conservative and are part of the ultra-right wing "America can do no wrong" crowd.

Twenty percent are fuzzy and confused in the middle. Can these numbers be true?

We have another saying in the Midwest about residing in the middle and straddling fences that deserves repeating here.

The story goes that a rancher went to the doctor because he cut his hand trying to remove a "post turtle" from the middle of a fence. The doc asked him what a "post turtle" was, and the rancher explained.

"When you are driving down a country road and you come across a fence post with a turtle balanced on top, that is a post turtle. You know he didn't get there by himself, he doesn't belong there, he can't get anything done while he's straddling the middle, and all you can do is help the poor, dumb thing get down."

Write me if you still can't decide about this election and are straddling the fence; perhaps, I can help.

October 18, 2008

The Flower of the Fallen, the Blood-Red Poppy, an Enduring Memorial Day Symbol

"In Flanders fields the poppies blow, between the crosses, row on row"

—COL. JOHN MCCRAE, 1915

Nothing, except perhaps the America flag, symbolizes Memorial Day more than the blood-red poppy.

And no one explained this symbol better than Colonel John McCrae, a Canadian veteran of World War I, who wrote a poem in 1915 entitled "In Flanders Fields."

His famous poem describes the bright red flowers that bloomed between the rows of white crosses that marked the graves of the war dead in Belgium. Those vivid reddish-orange flowers, poppies, were soon known throughout the Allied world as the "flower of the fallen," sometimes, "the flower of remembrance."

Although I have no live poppies in my yard like my mother used to have in her garden, I will never forget the reverent and simple pleasure of picking them for "Decoration Day."

I would love to find poppies to take to cemeteries on this Memorial Day weekend, but they are not readily available.

Luckily, I found an alternative flower choice while reading a Memorial Day speech transcript by Sylvia M. on www.usmemorial-day.org.

The idea came from an email the speaker had received from Sylvia Mohr. The idea: use fresh, red carnations, an inexpensive and available option, to decorate the graves of fallen soldiers and other loved ones.

Here is what Sylvia wrote about her idea and how she intends to use the carnations:

> This weekend I plan to do something different. I am going to buy some carnations each day and go to one of the nearby

cemeteries and walk through the sections for soldiers. When I find a grave that has no flowers, I'll leave one and say a prayer for the family of that person, who for some reason could not bring their soldier flowers. I will pray for our country and all who serve or have served. For their families, who also serve by losing precious days, weeks, and months spent with their loved ones who are off serving, preserving peace and the freedom we have in this country. I'll pray for the families who paid the ultimate price, whose loved ones died, or were taken captive and never returned. I'll pray for anyone who may still be in captivity and thinks perhaps they are forgotten. I do NOT forget.[17]

Poppies or carnations? It doesn't really matter.

What is important is why this tradition endures.

One can almost see the poppies blooming between the rows of white crosses on Flanders Field and hear the voices of the fallen as described in the final lines of Colonel McRae's World War I poem:

"We are the Dead. Short days ago / We lived, felt dawn, saw sunset glow, / Loved and were loved, and now we lie, / In Flanders fields. / Take up our quarrel with the foe: / To you from failing hands we throw / The torch; be yours to hold it high. / If ye break faith with us who die / We shall not sleep, though poppies grow / In Flanders fields."

May 27, 2010

Naked Politicians, Common Sense, and Clothing Advice

Clothes do indeed make the man, as the saying goes.

Mark Twain, who was known for wearing crisp, distinctive white suits, is credited with saying, "Clothes make the man. Naked people have little or no influence on society."

Neither do "naked" politicians.

It has long been my opinion that blustering congressmen on Capitol Hill, who love to preen and posture, are really "naked as a jaybird," whatever the word "jaybird" means exactly.

I am not speaking literally about clothes, at least, not yet. I'll get to that.

Right now, I am equating "naked" with their abhorrent lack of common sense.

In my way of thinking, such a pretentious sort of politician is just like the pompous ruler in the children's fairytale, "The Emperor's New Clothes." The portentous ones, not speaking here of the politicians who exhibit grace and humility, are the only ones who do not know that they are parading around without clothes.

The rest of us see their silly pontifications as just that—naked. If appearance counts, they apparently believe their own blustering.

Pardon me while I get off my soapbox about "naked" politicians who lack common sense, and let us return to Mark Twain's theory about clothes defining the person. The two are connected.

Look no further than Simon Cowell of *American Idol* fame. His signature attire is a simple tee shirt worn with jeans, as if to say with honesty, "I am wealthy beyond belief and I can wear anything I want." The late actress Katharine Hepburn was never ever seen without a high-collared shirt or blouse and a silk scarf. Her personal dress code defined her, giving an air of elegance and refinement. Perhaps, she was simply trying to cover her long neck and hide wrinkles. We'll never know, but it does not matter because we will always think of her as one classy lady.

Jackie Kennedy Onassis probably did more to create a signature look than most anyone with her pillbox hats and two-piece day dresses, the rage of the '60s. Her attire shouted out, "I am loving this outfit," and of course, every woman wanted one.

Dorothy Hamill, Olympic figure skater, wore a unique wedge haircut that now bears her name. All you have to say to your hairdresser is "I want a Dorothy Hamill," and you will have it. Her defining look achieved immortality.

Most folks know and understand what an Indiana Jones hat looks like, and most anyone over thirty-five needs no explanation of a J. R. Ewing Stetson.

The Queen Mother and her hats need no explanation either.

Each signature look carries with it a mighty statement about the individual.

So, it appears that we do, indeed, collectively subscribe to the idea that "You are what you wear." We may profess otherwise, but the truth is we all pay attention to how others look.

We may believe what we wear does not matter, but we know better. Erma Bombeck, beloved American humorist, is just grateful she lives in a society that wears clothes. Erma once observed, "I never leaf through a copy of National Geographic without realizing how lucky we are to live in a society where it is traditional to wear clothes."

And I might add—in a society where it is traditional to champion common sense.

May 20, 2006

Short Words Make People Say
What They Really Mean

"There is strength and force in short words, words that blast and boom, throb and thump, clank and chime, hiss and buzz and zoom. There is grace and charm in short words like lull and hush and purr. There are short lush words like dank, muck, and drench; and short dry ones like crisp, parch, and husk . . . give me words that pry and push, that slash and hack, that cut and clip, that chip and saw. Words are fun to fuss with, to stir and mix, and make work for you."

—WRITTEN DECADES AGO BY H. PHELPS GATES
of the *Christian Science Monitor*

My sentiments exactly, Mr. Gates. We could have used you during the presidential campaign of 2004.

Never have I heard such words as I did during the election of '04.

Soon, I came to realize that politics, indeed, has its own language. Some of that language is new this time around.

Did you notice, too? Perhaps not; slick words do tend to roll glibly over us.

You may have missed some of them. Oh, those silver-tongued devils!

Although determined to learn this exotic new language, I am forced to admit I do not speak their tongue well.

Increasingly, however, I became intrigued by the words which peppered the campaign's printed and spoken language (as though we know what those words mean).

Am I the only one who ran for the dictionary?

At any rate, they were all doing it—the news media, pundits, and countless authors, each with a brand new book filled with weighty analyses and theories.

So, I experimented with this phenomenon by watching all the major television networks and cable news networks, listened to talk radio, and bought or borrowed the latest political books.

I was so hooked I rarely cooked. (Forgot to mention broadcasters tend to rhyme, badly, I might add.)

I also noticed during my poll of pundits and politicians that they tended to use alliteration a lot.

Hence, my Primer for those Puzzled by Politics, Perturbed by Pundits, and Perplexed by Pontificators.

Note: alliteration was done mostly by telegenic (looking good on TV) news talk show hosts.

In light of all this, unabashedly, I offer a primer for the pained patrons of Politics 2004:

- culpable—You are acting guilty no matter what you say.
- soporific statement—Sleep-inducing, boring speech.
- "having said that"—Do you have to keep saying that?
- "I need a little time to get my arms around it"—I have no idea what you are talking about, and I have to get my research guys to figure this out.
- bloviate—Not in most dictionaries. Did Bill O'Reilly make this word up?
- conundrum—Why don't they just say "riddle"?
- exculpatory—Likely to prove someone is innocent, even though guilt is assumed first!
- copacetic—Excellent or good. Pundits can't possibly come right out and say anything is "good," can they?
- duplicitous—Deceitful, dishonest. What they would really like to say: "You double-dealing, two-faced, blankity, blank, blank." You get the idea.
- opined—To express an opinion. OK, I can use this one, but when I hear "opined" I keep thinking of "pining away for a lost love." Too much Emily Dickinson, perhaps. Never mind.

- impolitic—Unwise, misguided, ill-advised. What they really are saying is that they just don't know how to get along with those in power!
- illiberal—Narrow-minded, small-minded. "Bigot" would work nicely.
- egregious—Extraordinarily bad, flagrant. I actually like this word and may start to use it!
- poseur—Someone who dresses or behaves to impress others. The word is French. Hmmm.
- odious—Loathsome, detestable. Translation: that guy stinks!
- conterminous—Having a common boundary. Could we say "contiguous" instead because I know we all learned that in fifth grade social studies.
- vitriol, contentious, ingrate, contumacious—Hateful and nasty, touchy, ungrateful, stubbornly disobedient. How about just saying the guy is a jerk?
- ineluctable—Unavoidable (At first, I swear they said electable.)
- inveigh—To speak angrily in criticism. For example, "I am not being difficult, I am inveighing."
- inexorable—Unalterable, unavoidable, relentless, unchangeable. "The exchange between Chris Matthews and Zell Miller on MSNBC was inexorable." Personally, I think "entertaining" described it best.
- perfidy—Deceit. As in exit polls, perhaps.

Try checking these out for yourself: fatuous, desultory, pleonexia, and impunity. (I jotted these down in just one day listening to talk radio. Have a dictionary nearby when you listen. I'm warning you! Talk radio is great fun, granted, but one has to have a thesaurus handy.)

My all-time favorite is this wonderful word, "bollixed." Turns out it means "messed up."

It is actually a corruption of a Gaelic word. If you have been "bollixed" by someone that means that person has gone out of his/her way to mess you up.

Aristotle is credited with saying that "man is by nature a political animal," and he said that a long, long time ago.

Not looking for much to change on that point, but I have come to agree with Charles de Gaulle. America sort of liked him.

Remember? That was when America liked France, too.

De Gaulle said this about politics and all that goes with it, "I have come to the conclusion that politics are too serious a matter to be left to the politicians."

And perhaps too serious a matter to be left to the pundits and pronouncers of news.

August 27, 2005

Do You Remember D-Day?
Do Generations X, Y, and Z?

---

*"Normandy is marked by the landings. It is inscribed
in people's hearts, in memories, in stone, in rebuilding,
in memorial plaques, in street names, everywhere."*

—REV. RENE-DENIS LEMAIGRE, priest of Lisieux

Do you remember D-Day? It happened sixty-seven years ago this week, on June 6, 1944, to be exact. On that day, the world witnessed the Allied invasion of Normandy and the beginning of the liberation of Europe and the end of World War II.

But do we remember? Some of us do, or at least remember being told about it by our parents or grandparents, or we might remember studying it in school.

Some of us don't, however.

Most baby boomers, including myself, are the children of those who lived during the World War II era, and some are their grandchildren. It is the Generations X (born mid-'60s to 1982), Y (called Echo Boomers, born mid-1970s to mid-1990s), and Z (born approximately 1991 to the 2000s) that worry me. Do they know about D-Day? Are we doing our job in helping them remember?

Regrettably, this pivotal moment in history passed by this week with relatively little fanfare.

I find this sad.

Missouri native Gen. Omar Bradley, commander of the US First Army at Normandy, said after the war that he never failed to remember D-Day. "I have returned many times to honor the valiant men who died . . . every man who set foot on Omaha Beach was a hero."

Still, I wonder if generations two and three times removed from "the greatest generation that ever lived" remember or even know about

D-Day. Broadcast journalist Tom Brokaw coined the term, "The Greatest Generation" in his book of the same name published in 1998, saying, "It is, I believe, the greatest generation any society has ever produced."[18]

And what they did to preserve freedom for generations to follow, it seems to me, should have a little more "to do" made about it.

Brokaw's book discussed how that generation served, not for personal gain, but because they believed it was the right thing to do. These men and women came home after the war and set to work to make America the leader of the free world, a prosperous nation, and a superpower.

I wasn't exactly sure how much I remembered myself, so I began researching D-Day. It didn't take long for me to realize that I was "rusty" on the subject.

Here are some staggering facts and inspirational observations that I found that may astound you as well.

"What a plan," said British Prime Minister Winston Churchill addressing the House of Commons on June 6, 1944. "This vast operation is undoubtedly the most complicated and difficult that has ever taken place."[19]

Indeed it was.

More than 155,000 young Allied troops from the United States, Great Britain, and Canada waded through the chest-high water and climbed the cliffs to storm the beaches of Normandy, France.

Gen. Dwight D. Eisenhower sent these brave men into combat in Operation Overlord with these words:

"The eyes of the world are upon you; the hopes and prayers of liberty-loving people everywhere march with you. In company with our brave allies and brothers in arms on other fronts, you will bring about the destruction of the German war machine, the elimination of Nazi tyranny over the oppressed people of Europe, and security for ourselves in a free world. Your task will not be an easy one. . . . [but] the tide has turned; the free men of the world are marching together to victory."[20]

The beaches of Normandy were named with these code words: Juno, Gold, Omaha, Utah, and Sword.

Prior to the invasion, Allied forces practiced their roles for D-Day for months along the southern coast of England. Also, the Allies conducted a deception operation called Operation Fortitude aimed at misleading the Germans about the date and place of the actual D-Day invasion.

By August after the D-Day invasion in June, the 12th Army Group, comprised of four field armies, had swollen to more than 900,000 men and was the largest group of American soldiers to ever serve under one field commander. That commander was Gen. Omar Bradley, a native of Clark, Missouri, who graduated from Moberly High School.

D-Day numbers are staggering: 2,395 aircraft, 867 gliders, and 6,939 naval vessels. By June 11 (D-day plus 5 as it is called), there were 326,547 troops, 54,186 vehicles, and 104,428 tons of supplies that had been landed on the beaches of Normandy.

According to the British Portsmouth Museum, there were millions more men and women in the Allied countries who were involved in the preparations for D-Day. They played thousands of different roles, both in the armed forces and as civilians.

To commemorate these heroes, what can you do to remember and to pass on their legacy?

To begin, visit the National D-Day Memorial website at d-day.org or dday-overlord.com for a wealth of historical information.

Commemorate D-Day by watching the few movies and television shows available that attempt to illustrate the intensity of the invasion of Normandy: *Band of Brothers*, *The Big Red One*, *The Longest Day*, and *Saving Private Ryan*.

And most importantly, shake a hand of a veteran and say thank you to all who sacrificed their lives gladly for their neighbors and for us on that momentous day—June 6, 1944.

Let us not forget.

June 9, 2011

Cemetery Visit Takes a Turn
for the Better on Memorial Day

Normally, I don't "hang out" in cemeteries.

However, it is Memorial Day week, and we do such things.

I anticipated the upcoming and obligatory cemetery visit to be rather dreary, so I planned on hurrying through it.

Spend more time at Dad's grave than the others, of course, but allow enough time to make sure that his headstone is clean and there are no weeds growing around it, I reminded myself.

Just hurry and get out of there, I thought.

Make a quick "drive-by" tour of the graves of Grandma and Grandpa, Aunt Ida, Aunt Aggie, Uncle Dick, Cousin Al, Cousin Robert, Aunt Lizzie and Uncle Phil and their baby daughter Kathleen, and on and on. There would be several graves to visit.

The truck was abundantly filled with bedding plants (I like to use fresh flowers), a garden tool to chop weeds if needed, and two jugs of water. Quick work, I decided.

To avoid the frenzy of the Memorial Day weekend, I decided to go early in the week to the cemetery in northwest Missouri where my mother's family is buried. When I arrived at Maple Grove, I noted that I was alone there, not another "living soul" in sight. Usually when one goes to the cemetery on Memorial Day, it is a busy place with the lanes filled with cars, and the grounds dotted with folks laying wreaths and decorating headstones with flowers and American flags.

Not this time; I was early.

Besides being alone, there was another problem that surfaced. I could not find the location of the graves by myself without help from Mom or Grandma. Mom is not able, and Grandma is gone.

For my siblings and me when we were growing up, the precise location of headstones was on a need-to-know basis. We never thought we would ever use a cemetery map; we had Mom and Grandma. Besides, our primary job back then was to carry empty coffee cans covered with aluminum foil and filled with iris, peonies, and spirea to the designated graves.

Without doubt, Memorial Day appeared to be more meaningful for my mother and grandmother than it was for us kids. They cut only the best fresh flowers from our yard and arranged them beautifully in cans or jars. Their day was solemn yet joyous, honoring the fallen and departed; ours was celebratory, honoring the official entrance of the long-awaited summer.

But, back to my recent visit to the cemetery. The wind was blowing gently, the temperature pleasant, the sky sunny, the day perfect.

And thus, as I hunted graves for nearly two hours, I quickly forgot about my "search and drop off flowers and get out of there quick" mission.

Surprisingly, I was having a good time.

My dad's grave was easy to find, as I have been there many times. My grandparents' headstone, on the other hand, was more difficult to locate, and some cousins' and aunts' graves impossible. So impossible, in fact, that I had to call my cousin Judy to help me find Aunt Ida's grave. Turns out it is easy if one has a map.

Eventually, I finished the task that was no longer a task.

I took pictures with my iPhone as I wandered through the rows of graves. I took notes and made a map so the next generation would fare better than ours.

It was too important not to do so, and whether it came from the wind or the heavens, I understood the message I heard that day.

May 21, 2009

Family
and
Friends

"Throw in free shipping—we've got a deal!"

Honey, I Bought a Bridge

"Honey, I bought a bridge," my husband said as he walked through the kitchen door one summer evening nearly eleven years ago.

I asked him if he meant to say he had shrunk the kids, but no, he said that, in fact, he had bought a bridge.

Now I am thinking that surely, he must have said "fridge." Nope. He repeated it again, "I bought a bridge."

To which I replied, "Just out of curiosity, say if one wanted to buy a bridge, how would one go about doing that?"

"Got a great deal," he said.

I was thinking something along the lines of this, "Exactly why do we need a bridge?"

Instead of saying anything, I waited for the sure-to-come long-winded explanation.

Long story short, and believe me it was a long story, he said it was just too good a deal to pass up.

Seems as though his brother-in-law knew of a new bridge being put in somewhere along the Moniteau River in south central Missouri. The county gave the old bridge to the contractor and let him figure out how to dispose of it. The contractor had no need for an old steel bridge and told the folks in the area that he would sell it cheap if someone would haul it off.

"What a great deal," my husband continued. "Not only is there oak flooring still intact on the bridge, but guess what? There is a second bridge. It is actually the better of the two and has a plaque indicating that it was built in 1898."

Hey, what can you do? A deal like that does not come along just any old day.

Thereupon, we set out to find said bridge and figure out how to move it home.

Are you with me on this?

The best part of Mission Bring-Home-the-Bridge-We-Just-Bought was the woodland paradise scenery we found—gorgeous Ozark woods and clear streams.

Locating the bridge was the easy part. Deciding how to move it home was the conundrum.

The bonus bridge, only twenty-five feet long, would be simple to move. We could borrow Cousin Gene's trailer and haul it easily along the county roads and onto the interstate and home with no insurmountable difficulty.

Don't ask me how we loaded it.

Transporting the big bridge, sixteen feet wide and fifty feet long, was a brain teaser for sure. State law prohibits traveling the interstate with such a long load except for limited daylight hours. County roads are difficult to maneuver with curves and hills to negotiate.

Looks like we would now have to find a tractor truck with a low-boy trailer and hire the job done.

The cost of the bridges was mounting, the great deal gone.

Today, after eleven years of enjoying the view (from our breakfast room) of these two steel bridges in the field north of our house, I have no real complaints.

Can't say as much for the neighbors. The wildlife loves the bridges though.

I have watched a fox take a nap on one of the beams, cats hunt mice in the weeds that have grown up around the bridges, deer enjoy the salt lick beside them, and wild birds roost on the girders.

I have to say I am somewhat at peace with my own Bridges of Lafayette County after all this time.

For a while there, "The" bridges, as we have named them, drove me crazy, and I even tried to sell them on eBay once. No bids whatsoever. I ran ads in magazines and told every contractor I knew about them.

Yesirree Bob, there's a sucker born every minute. And we are it.

By the way, I have a couple of bridges that are always on the market. So, pass the word. I can make you a great deal!

May 27, 2006

Jokester Gene Runs in the Family

On April Fools' Day, I foolishly assumed that I would survive the day unscathed because the offspring who used to play the practical jokes around here have flown the nest.

Not to be. Grandson Halen came running across the yard to tell me there was a big red fox at the edge of the woods. Since he is young and presumably innocent, his was an absolutely believable story. Besides, the fox usually appears around this time of year anyway. I wanted to believe him because I had not seen the fox this spring. He usually shows up by now, so off I went to the woods to look for myself.

Meanwhile, from behind, I hear giggles and a small voice yelling, "April Fools!"

Wonderful, I think to myself. Here we go again. As the sayings go, "the apple does not fall far from the tree" or "like father, like son." Both apply here.

Let us just say I have seen this movie.

Halen's father, in his day, was masterful at tricking me. He took great pride in this. In fact, he found it to be so much fun that he decided to make it a year-long event.

April Fools' Day was not enough for him. Oh no. His pranks often turned into a long-running mini-series of ruses, such as "The Great Pineapple Caper."

His very first practical joke should have been warning enough. He came running into the house that day, obviously wounded, with his hand wrapped in a towel. Blood was everywhere. Naturally, I began basic first aid, whereupon I soon discovered the blood to be catsup.

He should have been in the movies. I should have seen what was coming.

From that moment on his chicanery progressed into an elaborate and quite ingenious hoax, all of which I swallowed.

Keven convinced me over time that he could taste the difference between different brands of pineapple and could tell the difference between off-brands and Dole.

He started his deception by telling me one evening at dinner, "This pineapple upside-down cake tastes different."

The next week, it was this: "Something in the fruit salad tastes funny. I think it is the pineapple."

He played this well and would wait a few weeks before he commented that the pineapple in whatever dish I made that day tasted fine now and must be Dole.

He said he knew what had been wrong with the pineapple earlier. He claimed he could tell if I used a name brand or an off-brand whether it was in the pineapple-orange salad, the cheesy fruit salad with pineapple, or the pineapple cream cheese dip.

"Keven, no one can tell the difference between pineapple brands," I finally yelled in frustration.

The thing was that he was always correct. He could indeed tell the brand, apparently by taste.

I could never figure out how.

This went on for months, and he never missed.

One day when he thought I was napping, I walked into the kitchen and noticed the light on in the pantry. There I found him going through the trash looking for the empty can of pineapple. I had made a fruit salad earlier in the day, and it had pineapple in it. He found the can.

Well, let us just say he was not Johnny Carson's The Great Carnac after all.

What a scoundrel, but he is not alone.

Ancient Rome had a spring holiday for practical jokes—the Festival of Hilarity, a day of honoring foolishness.

Likewise, the French call April 1 their April Fish festival. School children tape a picture of a fish on someone's back, crying "April Fish" (*Poisson d'Avril*) until the prank is discovered.

Historians tell us that April Fools' Day originated because Pope Gregory XIII created a new calendar changing New Year's Day from April 1 to January 1. Some folks refused to accept the new date and continued to celebrate the New Year on April 1. Then others began to make fun of the people who celebrated on January 1 by sending them on "fool's errands" or tricking them with practical jokes.

Around our household, we do not need a special holiday to fool people. Ours is ongoing. I have learned one thing though. Always check the trash.

April 7, 2007

Mother-of-the-Groom Advice:
Shut up and Wear Beige

As I browsed the internet trying to find advice for mothers-of-the-groom (since I am about to be one in mere days), I ran across an interesting story published some time ago, in *USA Today*.

Craig Wilson wrote about how mothers-of-the-groom are not wearing beige anymore (more like hot pink) and about how they are taking a more active part in wedding planning (as in giving advice). He discussed how the role of mother-of-the-groom is changing with regard to wedding do's and don'ts.

Remember the old adage for mothers-of-the-groom: wear tan, sit in the back, and don't ask any questions or offer any answers.

Advice more commonly referred to as "wear beige and keep your mouth shut!"

I get it; however, I am wearing jade green and have never been known to keep my mouth shut.

I could be doomed already.

And what if I am called upon to make a toast or a short speech? I need to practice, so you, dear readers, get to be my guinea pigs.

Here, then, is my advice (first rough draft) for my sweet kids, the lovely bride and dashing groom:

- Don't marry for money; you can borrow it cheaper.
- Hey kids, I am so old that I can remember when the air was clean and sex was dirty.
- Love is like a mushroom. You never know if it's the real thing until it's too late.

OK, maybe not that kind of advice. I'll start over:

- Behold the turtle that makes progress only when he sticks his neck out.

- If you want a place in the sun, you've got to expect a few blisters.
- Compromise is the art of dividing a cake so that everybody believes that he or she got the biggest piece.
- Swallowing angry words is much easier than having to eat them.
- May you always be the kind of person your dog thinks you are.

Too trite, perhaps? I will begin again.
- For the bride: remember that when he asks if he can change the TV channels, no matter how you answer, it is going to sound like "yes" to him.
- For the groom: If a woman says, "Do it when you get a minute" that really means "It should have been done already and without me telling you."

You know what, on second thought, I think I will just sit in the back and keep my mouth shut.

September 17, 2009

When the AC Goes out, So Does Good Humor

"What dreadful hot weather we have!
It keeps me in a continual state of inelegance."

—JANE AUSTEN

Did you know that pasta can lose its shape when your air conditioning quits?

Did you know that chocolate actually turns gray in high humidity if you don't put it in the refrigerator?

I didn't know that either, but I found out last weekend when our air conditioning unit decided to "meet its maker" after twenty-two years of near-perfect service.

The resulting hot and humid ordeal lasted three-plus days.

It is undoubtedly written somewhere that air conditioning breakdowns are required to occur over a holiday weekend.

You guessed it—our AC breakdown happened over the Fourth of July. We were at the Lake of the Ozarks where typically one cannot find a repairman if the fish are biting or if there is a cloud in the sky. In this case, the repairmen did his best to get there, but we were simply too far down the list of "you have to come now" service requests. He didn't make it.

Did you know that when you live three days in record heat and humidity without AC, your bread molds overnight and everything in your house attracts dust by the bucketload?

The dust was about the only thing that hung around our house. Some guests started bailing out on the second day, and I don't blame them at all.

Our immediate family stayed, however, and so did a cousin from Nashville and a nephew from Kansas. I really don't know why. I was ready to leave on the second day myself.

Instead, they accepted their fate and dug in for the duration.

My solution—I jumped in the lake and stayed there until forced to come inside for food.

I did not want to cook, and left that up to my cousin from the South who did. Incidentally, the sweltering temperatures in the kitchen never deterred him for a second.

When the rest of us woke on the morning after the third stifling night, we found our Nashville cousin in the kitchen frying sausage to add to his homemade gravy and baking biscuits in, yes, the oven!

"Hey, good morning," he said. "This heat isn't so bad. The pioneers never had air conditioning, so I guess we don't need it either."

"Hey," I replied, "you know what Benjamin Franklin said, don't you? 'After three days, fish and visitors stink.'"

I guess you could say I was a lot like Jane Austen about then—in a continual state of inelegance and bad humor.

My cousin, who always seems to be in a disgustingly good mood, laughed as he started frying up some bacon to accompany the biscuits and gravy.

I went outside where there was a breeze and ate a popsicle.

July 8, 2010

When the Landline Phone Rings, Do Not Answer

"I don't answer the phone. I get the feeling whenever I do that there will be someone on the other end."

—FRED COUPLES

Our home landline phone was ringing the other night and that in itself was such an oddity I thought I had better answer it, something I am generally loath to do.

It was my grandson Halen.

He and the telemarketers are about the only ones who use our landline anymore. So, it has to be one of the two. Occasionally, someone will look us up in the phone book and call, but that occurrence is rare. Almost all our incoming calls go to our cell phones these days, and such is the way of the world.

BTW (meaning "by the way" in grandkid lingo), I cannot wait for Halen to get a cell phone.

This grandma is lobbying his parents for a cell phone for him. Then he can call me anytime, anywhere, and I will answer without dread that the call could be from a telemarketer, political push poll operative, or from my credit card company offering the latest, greatest deal on balance transfers.

OK, about now you are wondering why in the world do we not use an answering machine or why don't we get voice mail? Simple answers: the answering machine died, and we have never replaced it. And, for the life of him, my husband cannot retrieve the voice mail messages, as he freely admits, because he is a bit technology-challenged. We gave up on both.

Yesterday, our cordless landline phone died, too. Realizing that we probably do need a landline of some kind or other, I went to the boxes in the basement to search. Surely there was an old one down there somewhere.

I found one son's cordless phone that he used in his undergrad college days. It is a high-tech thing with a keypad I cannot understand. I was able to charge the battery, but could not get the darn thing to ring. I read the instruction book very carefully and so did the techno-challenged hubby. No luck for either of us.

Husband said, "Do you want me to take this phone to work and see if someone can figure it out?" I said no, that I would call the son because surely he could talk me through it over the phone. I used my cell to call him.

"Mom," he said. "This phone operates with a joystick technology. It is very simple. Just use it like you would a joystick on a video game."

Like I would know how to do that, I am thinking.

So, there you go. It is simpler to not answer the phone.

I recall what Ogden Nash once said about middle age and phones: "Middle age is when you are sitting at home on a Saturday night and the phone rings and you hope it isn't for you."

October 23, 2008

The Final Neighborhood Garage Sale is Never the Last (Or . . . "Hubby Covets Neighbor's Garage Sale Trash")

"So that you'll never be tempted to participate in a neighborhood garage sale, allow me to explain how they go. Friday night you're up until two in the morning marking prices on all the junk you're hoping people will buy. At this point you're almost psychotically optimistic, calculating the total value of your inventory at slightly over twenty-two thousand dollars."

—W. Bruce Cameron, author, columnist, and humorist

My neighbors and I are planning our "final" garage sale.

Thus, a definition of the word "final" might be in order here. According to Encarta Encyclopedia, the word means "the last of a number or series of similar things." Final also means conclusive and allowing no further discussion.

Such as involving a garage sale, the last garage sale, in fact, that my neighbors and I will ever have.

We mean it this time, too. No one believes us.

We are deadly serious, though, because the upcoming fall sale will be conclusively the last, positively the last, and without a shadow of a doubt, the last garage sale! There will be no further discussion of this either, we neighbors agree.

But we lie. Here's the proof.

Neighbor, we'll call her Susan, once signed a pledge written by her husband promising to never again hold or participate in a yard or garage sale or any other kind of rummage sale. Another neighbor, let's call her Kathy, announced clearly and adamantly that she was finished, done, spent. No more garage sales for her. The third neighbor, we'll name her Sandy, was too busy and was simply running out of things to sell and, yes, running out of interest, too.

Yet, we are doing it again.

One of the neighbors, not to be mentioned by name, was well ahead of the rest of us. Early on, she began the process of dragging her basement treasures to the garage thus forcing her husband to park outside days ahead of the sale. Her garage was overflowing with clothes racks, tables, and miscellaneous "like-new, priced-to-sell" household items, so naturally, there was no room for a car. Makes perfect sense to me. Meanwhile, my husband, who incidentally never fails to notice anything that could possibly be free-of-charge, observed that said neighbor was cleaning out her house and bringing lots of non-worthy garage sale items to the curb for the morning trash pickup.

He began to covet her trash, in particular, stacks of empty plastic five-gallon buckets.

When I called to ask about the buckets, my neighbor's husband answered the phone. "Could hubby have them?" I asked him.

"He wouldn't want them, they aren't any good. I drilled holes in them to water flowers," came the reply.

Five minutes later my spousal unit was in their driveway snatching the buckets in the dark of night. He reported back to me that they were perfect for carrying boards, tools, bricks, and rocks, and would work just fine.

Of course, they would, I thought, and they will work just fine in my garage sale in the spring, too.

That is, of course, if I have a garage sale, you understand.

September 9, 2009

Flocked by Flamingoes

"See how the sacred old flamingoes come, painting with shadows all the marble steps. Aged and wise they seek their wanted perches."

—**WILLIAM BUTLER YEATS**

Their preferred perch apparently was our front yard, as last week a flock of flamingoes landed there.

We were "flocked."

Simply put, that means that early one morning we discovered a flock of hot pink and chartreuse flamingoes perching on our lawn, some on one leg, some bent and pecking through blades of grass.

If plastic flamingoes can peck, that is. It was indeed a sight to behold.

Along with the brightly colored birds was a banner indicating a phone number to call if you happened to be the recipient of the flock. A message inside a plastic bag hung on our front door mentioned that the flock would migrate if you were kind enough to donate to the flock's cause, in this case a church youth group. Additionally, you could text a number when you put your donation in the bag, and the flock would then miraculously leave and fly to a friend's house of your choosing.

We were happy to oblige, especially the part about sending the flock to a friend's house.

I knew instantly who that would be, too, because it was flamingo practical joke payback time. I had waited a long time for this moment (Machiavellian laugh here).

This friend had a flamingo joke coming.

It seems that for a reason known only to her, she decided it would be fun to place pink flamingoes in our yard on my birthday, on my husband's birthday, in the winter, on Easter Sunday, on the Fourth of

July, or on Christmas Eve. Any holiday, she thought, would be a good time for a flamingo to land in our front yard, back yard, in the trees, on the porch, in the driveway.

Let me tell you, those flamingoes popped up everywhere around us. The problem—we did not know at the time who was behind the clever caper. Once I ran an ad in the paper offering a reward for information leading to the discovery of the flamingo perpetrator. I questioned neighbors, relatives, and friends. No one had a clue, or they played dumb.

Over a period of several months we found the following in or around our yard: three hot pink Beanie Babies, three light pink flamingo stir sticks made of pipe cleaners and dyed cotton balls and stuck in a bucket of sand, one tacky, exceptionally tacky, pink flamingo paper weight, one Keepsake flamingo ornament titled "lawn patrol" (not so bad), Easter baskets filled with toy flamingoes and hot pink plastic eggs, and a book called *What Makes Flamingos Pink?*

The mystery was killing me until one day, out of the blue, my neighbor couldn't take the guilt any longer and made a tactical error, as criminals are wont to do. We received an anonymous postcard in the mail showing real flamingoes standing on one foot, of course, in a resort pool at some unknown tropical location.

It was then I remembered that our neighbors were on vacation in Mexico.

Criminals always leave a clue.

Therefore, and as we speak, she has a flock of plastic flamingoes, a big flock, in her yard!

One worrisome thought occurs to me, however. I hope she doesn't change her *modus operandi* and start sending us plastic pigs or goats.

July 29, 2010

Genealogy, Arsenic, and Old Lace

"Every family tree has some sap in it."

—UNKNOWN

I guess you could say I was never into genealogy that much, although my mother was passionate about it and researched our ancestors with fervor for more than twenty years.

Funny how time changes us, though. Now I rather like it. Many of us think we came over on the *Mayflower* and own a castle in Scotland, right?

Sooner or later, most of us start to shake our family tree for one reason or another and hope no lemons, nuts, or bad apples fall out.

In my case, I found more than a little sap.

My research began because my sister found an old picture of our great-great grandfather and sent it to my brother. Curious, he began researching one Louis Ferree Carothers, a captain in the Union Army, who was born on November 14, 1816, and left this life on July 13, 1871.

We assumed that our mother surely wrote more about him in her family history, "The Kreek-Carothers Family," compiled in 1983. My copy was somewhere in a box in the basement, left there untouched all this time.

Eventually, I found it and discovered some relatives that made me swell with pride.

And sure enough, I found that the Carothers family (also spelled Carruthers or Caruthers) did indeed hale from Scotland, although originally from France.

And yes, they once owned a castle.

I learned that the Carruthers Castle is located somewhere near Dumfriesshires, Scotland, but is now in ruins.

Then, I found two more Carruthers Castles, one called Lochmaben and the other Comlongon Castle, this one with a lady ghost.

Shaking the family tree was getting better and better.

I began to wonder if we had a king hiding in that tree somewhere and decided it was worth a deeper look.

Who said genealogy was not fun? Me, I think.

Never mind that. Starting with my great-great grandfather, Lewis Ferree, I traced his roots past the Revolutionary War to our common ancestor, Capt. John Carothers, a judge and member of the General Assembly. John was born in 1739 and died at his family home in East Penn Borough Township, Cumberland County, Pennsylvania, on February 26, 1798.

The circumstances of his death, however, were far from ordinary.

Instead, what I discovered buried within my mother's stacks of notes and genealogical files, was a chilling tale of double murder, a story filled with insane jealousy, arsenic, and yes, lace.

If you are interested, here is the shortened version.

It seems as though a young girl named Sarah Clark (nicknamed Sally) came to live with the John Douglas family, who were friends and neighbors of John and Mary Carothers, my ancestors.

Sarah "contracted a strong attachment" for Mr. Douglas's son, who was at that time paying attention to Miss Ann Caruthers, daughter of John and Mary.

Are you with me so far?

Overcome with her infatuation (what we would describe today as "fatal attraction"), Sarah "determined to destroy the life of Ann Carothers and gain the object of her affections."

Following her clever and sinister plan, she was hired on as a servant in the Carothers house and "bided her time." She wore servant's attire, a dark dress trimmed in white lace.

The historical account reads, "Having no ill will against the family, she desired to poison only Ann Carothers, and with this in view, she purchased some arsenic. With no suitable opportunity offering, she grew desperate and put the arsenic in a pot of leaven."

I am sure you guessed it by now; the family all ate the bread and became sick.

Capt. John Carothers died quickly, followed soon afterwards by his wife Mary. Andrew Carothers, Ann's brother, lived but was a cripple for life.

Ann Carothers, the intended victim, was the only survivor and never married.

Sarah, a.k.a. Sally, was tried, convicted as a murderess witch, and hanged at Carlisle, Pennsylvania, or so the story goes.

Incidentally, I did not find any *Mayflower* passengers or kings in my mother's genealogy tales.

Just murder, she wrote.

March 31, 2011

For Men, Haggling Over
the Price is Like Hunting

"How low can you go?" my husband asked the furniture sales clerk.

"What do you mean? This price is rock bottom already," responded the salesman.

Meanwhile, I am hiding behind a potted ficus tree somewhere in the gymnasium-size furniture showroom in utter chagrin and unending embarrassment.

The price haggling between these two had been going on awhile.

They were beginning to look like two bull elks locking horns.

The salesman continued, "Hey, it is only money and you cannot take it with you. You know those caskets don't have side pockets on them."

"I'll make you a deal," my husband retorted. "If you were to sell it today, would you take two hundred dollars less than the sticker price for the kitchen table and four chairs and the bedroom set combined—one price, one package deal?"

The furniture-shopping excursion was an attempt to help our recently graduated son find apartment furniture. Now, the son was strolling away nonchalantly trying to pretend he did not know either of us, me hiding behind the tree and his dad growing increasingly boisterous as he moved in for the kill.

If up to me, I quietly observed, I am more interested in the shopping experience itself rather than the competition. This war of the cave men is no fun!

We women love to feel the furniture, sit on it, match it to paint swatches, and consider accessories that may be critically important to the finished look of the room.

Not a man, not a hunter.

It was then I realized that the battle going on between these two males was all about winning and making a quick, decisive kill, not about the furniture itself.

"Well, I will have to ask my manager. Besides you are already getting the sale price," continued the salesman.

After several moments passed, my husband's adversary returned with the final verdict.

"OK. We can sell it to you for fifty dollars less than the sale price but that is it, as low as I can go."

Thinking we were near the end of the bartering, I was disheartened beyond measure when my husband replied in a firm, I've-got-you-now voice, "What about this ad in the paper I have right here that says buy one item, get the second one thirty percent off?"

"Does not apply to sets," said the sales guy quicker than a duck on a June bug. "The table and chairs are a set and so is the headboard, bed frame, and chest. Sorry, you cannot use the coupon on this."

Whereupon, my husband did not miss a beat. "Throw in free shipping and we've got a deal."

They shook hands, and I have no idea who really won. It was all about the dance and the struttin' anyway.

Next time, I am buying online.

May 15, 2008

Time Flies Too Fast

When I was in the eighth grade, our teacher asked the class to explain a phrase she wrote on the blackboard.

The phrase: "Time flies." No one could.

The teacher smiled and quietly replied, "You can't. They fly too fast!"

None of us were ready for her surprising answer, and incidentally, the entire class missed the point.

We thought she meant that time flies by fast, so quickly that one is surprised, not that we should try to time pesky flies with a stopwatch, for example.

It was an important lesson I learned about life that day, and it had nothing to do with flies. The lesson is this: in school or in life, we are never ready for the punch line.

And that leads me to the rest of my story, as the late Paul Harvey, master of punch lines, would say.

Nearly fifty kids were packed into this teacher's basement classroom in a small Missouri town when I was in the eighth grade. It was 1961. Learning was exciting that year, as we were enthralled with the teacher's stories of her real-life experiences during World War II. We learned history firsthand from her account of serving as a Red Cross captain attached to an army unit on the Yugoslav-Italian border. She told us of attacks by guerrilla fighters, stories about prisoners of war, and of flying over Mount Vesuvius in an open-door cargo plane.

Most of us were amazed at the teacher's in-depth knowledge of almost any subject. She taught history, English, math, science, and physical education without benefit of computers or a SMART Board.

She held advanced degrees, but never spoke of them. Her vast knowledge spoke to us instead.

When our class moved from that basement room upstairs to the high school, this teacher moved with us. There she taught geography, world history, or American history to most of us at some time or other.

Over the years I saw her often. About two years ago she came to our house for a holiday dinner, one of the last times she was able to leave the nursing home where she is currently a resident.

This coming January 1st, she will celebrate her ninety-third birthday. Yet, she does not know one day from another. She looks at her grandchildren and asks to be introduced. She can't remember to eat, and she repeats herself every few seconds if she talks at all.

When I visit her, she tells me her father is outside the window and I should let him in, that her mother is sick and she needs to go home to take care of her, that her husband is fixing a bird house in the backyard, and when he is done they are leaving before the roads get too bad. Sometimes, she says I just missed seeing her cousins.

All of these people are dead, incidentally, but she talks about them as if they were sitting beside us.

Her world is a radius of twelve inches around her. If you are farther away than that, she may not see or hear you. She doesn't know where she is, or whether it is Sunday or Thursday, or if it is raining.

Rarely, do I see a glimmer of that teacher who once knew so much.

And of course, she doesn't remember her stunning punch line she delivered many years ago, "Time flies! You can't. They fly too fast!"

But I do. How could I forget, because that teacher who taught me then and who taught me all my life is my mother?

Once in a while she still surprises me with a punch line that I never expect.

The other day, when the residents of her special care unit were acting out and were very rebellious and noisy, she looked at me and said with complete clarity, "Kay Jean, get out of here while you can."

Time does indeed fly too fast.

September 9, 2010

You Are Never Too Old
for a Summer Road Trip

---

*"Twenty years from now you will be more disappointed by the
things that you didn't do than by the ones you did do. So throw off
the bowlines. Sail away from the safe harbor. Catch the trade
winds in your sails. Explore. Dream. Discover."*

—MARK TWAIN

A clue that I love road trips is the packed bag sitting on my closet
floor, just in case the opportunity to travel cross-country or anywhere
else presents itself.

I blame this trait on my parents.

You see, they loved to travel and believed that seeing unfamiliar
locales via the open road was a vital part of childhood education. So
do I.

Thus, that was a good enough reason for me to "suggest" quite
recently that our two young adult single sons accompany us, mom
and dad, on a road trip west. They have done this before and know
the drill. Yet, I worried that they are not kids anymore and might
not be thrilled at the idea. My husband tried guilt to coerce them,
saying, "Boys, this could be the last time the four of us take a road
trip together."

I was thinking, "You have to be kidding; I plan on making them
take us when we're eighty-eight."

Admittedly, they might have a reasonable fear of boredom and
embarrassment at the idea of traveling with their parents. Yet, they
embraced the road trip good-naturedly, probably because they come
by wanderlust naturally.

In my youth, back in the '50s and early '60s, it was not unusual for
the boys' grandfather to come home from work on a Friday evening

and announce happily, "We are going to Colorado in the morning. Do you have a bag packed?"

I learned to have mine ready.

Sometime between three o'clock and five o'clock the following morning, our family would leave our Missouri River bottom farm home for Colorado or California or other parts out west (sans automobile air conditioning and thus the night travel).

For some reason, we never went east, and I have yet to figure out why. Summer after summer, we headed west toward the mountains with all our shoes piled in one open cardboard box in the back of our green woody Desoto station wagon.

Another box held a loaf of white bread and cans of Spam, apples, cookies, and a jug of water for a noon picnic at a roadside park. We thought it a feast.

Those roadside parks, by the way, were usually located next to a historical marker, and I am quite certain we stopped at every one of them between Kansas City and the Pacific Ocean. That is, if my mom, a history teacher in her day job, had anything to say about it. My dad was the photographer for the trips, lining us up in front of countless such markers, and when we stopped at gas stations, he treated each of us to a bottle of soda pop (as long as we did not fight too much in the backseat). Mostly, we read road signs and jingles, sang songs, quibbled some, and laughed a lot.

A family squeezed together in a hot car on long road trips with only each other for company sears unforgettable memories into one's psyche.

I guess I was hoping to create the same memories with our sons before they spread their wings and fly too far away.

We didn't leave at 3:00 a.m., although my husband wanted to, and we did not eat Spam and white bread (it wouldn't have surprised me if he wanted to do that, too). I never made the boys stand in front of one historical marker, although I almost did in a fleeting, nostalgic weak moment.

I guess I look at this road trip as a practice run for when we are eighty-eight and the offspring get an urgent phone call from us asking, "Boys, do you have your bag packed? We are leaving for Colorado in the morning, and oh, by the way, will you drive us?"

August 13, 2009

Remembering Burma-Shave Signs

"Farewell O verse, along the road. How sad to see, you're out of mode."

—Burma-Shave

It is mid-August, and that fact alone takes me back to my youth when almost everyone took a vacation in the month of August. School didn't start until after Labor Day; baseball was over for the summer, and swimming lessons were completed.

Time to pack up the woody station wagon and head west.

From Missouri, we traveled the now-storied Route 66 with no idea that it was anything special at all, just another long, hot road to Grandma's house in California.

In the '50s, my parents drove us kids cross-country every August in a car the size of a boat with only an AM radio and no air conditioning. As I recall, when we crossed the desert from Phoenix to San Diego, it was by night with bags of water tied to the car to cool the radiator.

I know some of you baby boomers will remember similar trips, and I will bet you remember Burma-Shave signs that dotted the highways as well.

We read them with delight and anticipation on those trips, and when we spotted a row of red signs in the distance, everyone in the car came to full alert lest we miss one.

We read them out loud in unison:

"Use this cream a day or two. Then don't call her. She'll call you," Burma-Shave.

Or this one, "These signs we gladly dedicate to men who've had no date of late."

By the time the mid-1960s arrived, the Burma-Shave signs were about to complete nearly three decades of success.

Antique collectors say that in its prime, Burma-Shave displayed seven thousand of the bright red signs, usually at least five in a row, to entertain travelers heading west.

But I digress. Back to some Burma-Shave jingles I love to remember.

"Past schoolhouses, take it slow. Let the little shavers grow," Burma-Shave.

Or, "When the stork delivers a boy, our whole darn factory jumps for joy."

Eventually, Burma-Shave signs spread to almost every state, with only Massachusetts receiving no signs at all. Too many trees might obstruct the view of signs there, I am told. A few other states had only a handful.

Besides serving as an ingenious advertising tool, Burma-Shave signs also offered guidance on societal issues.

"Many a forest used to stand where a lighted match got out of hand," Burma-Shave.

And this one, "If daisies are your favorite flower, keep pushin' up those miles-per-hour."

At the end of its glorious run in 1963, Burma-Shave offered its final rhyme: "Farewell O verse, along the road. How sad to see, you're out of mode," Burma-Shave.

August 19, 2010

Childhood Friends—A Good Barometer for the Future

Tell your children and grandchildren to pay attention now to their friends and acquaintances. They will meet them again in the next life. By that I mean, when they reach their adult life, childhood will seem like a faintly-remembered past life, but don't be fooled—old childhood acquaintances will be there just the same.

They are now disguised as people you think you have never met. For example, Susie is now Melanie.

She's the one that turned the tables on you in first grade. She's still at it, only now she's your co-worker operating under another name.

Remember when you dropped your favorite bracelet on the playground? Susie picked it up and wore it. You told the teacher, but too late. Susie had already been there and said you stole it from her first and she was just taking it back.

Now, Melanie is stealing your idea at work and claiming she thought of it first.

Then, there's Beverly, Jeri, Janet, and Paula who liked you then and never believed that you stole Susie's bracelet anyway. They knew it was yours. They are still around, only now their names are Beth, Kathy, Linda, and Marsha.

As time marches on, I am continually surprised by the people I meet in life.

I don't know why I should be.

They invariably remind me of someone from my youth.

Some support you, some let you down, some defend you, some will never forgive you, some are kind when you most need it, and some sense your weakness and kick you in the gut.

Tell your children and grandchildren, this never changes.

One of the hidden benefits of aging is that it is so easy now to understand these folks because I can call them by a given name. I have already met them in a past life—childhood.

I can simply tell my mother, brother, sister, or old friends (who were there at the time), that Melanie is just like Susie. Sam is just like Alan.

They get it instantly. All is understood.

I don't even have to give them the details.

However, if anything gets too weird or if you think those around you are behaving insanely, take the advice of Rita Mae Brown who says, "The statistics on sanity are that one out of every four Americans is suffering from some form of mental illness. Think of your three best friends. If they are okay, then it's you!"[21]

July 9, 2005

Alzheimer's, a Season of "Lasts"

"Old age comes on suddenly, and not gradually as is thought."

—EMILY DICKINSON

Most stories about Alzheimer's catch my eye, but none more than one I read this past week, a *USA Today* story about a family's ongoing blog about Alzheimer's.

I am interested in this because my mother, ninety-four, was officially diagnosed with Alzheimer's more than twelve years ago. We have been in the throes of this dreaded disease ever since, so naturally I am interested in everything Alzheimer's. And I must admit, I worry about getting it myself.

The story mentioned above is named simply "Bob's Blog," a personal journal kept in association with *USA Today*. It is about Bob Blackwell, sixty-nine, a retired, once-brilliant, highly talented CIA analyst who was diagnosed with early-onset Alzheimer's five years ago.

At first, he started writing about his battle with the illness, but soon thereafter, his wife Carol took over blogging about their personal journey.

She tells poignant, sometimes humorous, and always loving tales about their daily lives. Recently, Carol has been writing the blog they keep for *USA Today* about "the season of lasts—listing things Bob has done for the last time. He has been a lifelong fan of University of Georgia football, for instance, but following the games last fall was too challenging."

And on and on the list of "lasts" continues.

Carol writes, "Here we are, and there's no cure and no promise of a cure . . . I know it's too late for a cure for Bob, the disease has moved into many parts of his brain, but I'm praying for my children and grandchildren. We have to find a cure."

If you are close to someone who is afflicted with Alzheimer's, I imagine that you drink in every word as well on the subject of finding a cure for future generations and for ourselves.

Unfortunately, the very definition of Alzheimer's is indeed foreboding.

Health reporter Janice Lloyd describes Alzheimer's as "a form of dementia that causes progressive loss of intellectual and social skills, the only disease among the top killers for which there is no prevention, cure, or treatment that will slow its progression."

We hear constantly in the news these days that the disease is thought to run in families, and the growth of Alzheimer's, the projected number of people over the age of sixty-five in the US, is now in the millions.

WebMD further explains, "About five to eight percent of adults over age sixty-five have some form of dementia. This percentage doubles every five years after sixty-five. As many as half of people in their eighties have some dementia."[22]

I find better news in the fact that new efforts are being made to raise public awareness, provide more funding for research, and speed up the timeline to find a cure.

And even better news is the fact that once in a while our loved ones with Alzheimer's emerge ever so briefly from the fog and come back, sometimes long enough for us to catch a glimmer of the person we used to know.

For example, the other day I could not get my mother to open her eyes. It was lunchtime at the special care Alzheimer's unit where she resides.

I tried to entice her to smell and taste her food and to take a sip of coffee, which incidentally she has adored her entire life.

It was the coffee I gave her that I believe brought her back to life. Right away, she opened her eyes and smiled. Then she squealed, "Oooooo, coffee. That's good." She then turned to a neighbor at the dining table and said, "Have you met my mother?" pointing to me.

Looking at me she said, "Kay Jean (the name she has always called me) have you met my mother?"

And that is how it goes most days, but this particular day she recognized the smell and taste of coffee and said, "Ooooo, that's good," and for ever so briefly, she was back.

January 19, 2012

The Joy
of
Technology

"Don't worry, I have it written down."

Boomers Are Gadgety Geniuses These Days

"For a list of all the ways technology has failed to improve the quality of life, please press three."

—ALICE KAHN

Who wants to be left behind when it comes to mastering the latest electronic gadgets?

Not baby boomers.

Think again in case you believe in the prevalent myth that baby boomers are techno phobic and cannot master high tech electronics.

Truth is we boomers love our gadgets so much that we are actually becoming good at them.

Evidence supporting this trend is all around us.

For instance, I recently observed a high-tech eighty-something couple at the outlet mall. They were walking through a store talking to each other on their bluetooth earpieces. Quite the sight, and yes, I have to admit, hip.

Hip octogenarians! Who knew?

Additionally, there are a growing number of savvy baby boomers that can text, surf, YouTube, iPhone, Blackberry, IM, and GPS with the best of them. Even the Wii is hot for seniors.

Baby boomer Steve practices golf on the Golden Tee video game in arcades. He enjoys the exercise, except for one time when he swung the wand a bit too hard and dislocated his thumb. We won't count him. Seriously though, there is a little game of golf that actually fits in your smart phone and may be safer than playing it in the arcade if you get into it as much as Steve. The game unbelievably holds four complete 18-hole golf courses in a handheld device.

Beautiful scenery. Blue skies. Mobile relaxation. No green fees!

My friend Beth has a new Blackberry, and let me tell you, she can text message using predictive text like a thirteen-year-old. My sister Pat has mastered IM (instant messaging) lingo.

Even my technologically challenged husband can maneuver his way through a cell phone menu, most of the time, that is. Granted, he cannot retrieve voice mail yet, but soon. We are hopeful.

I am impressed with this cool, "chichi" (trendy) technology. Might as well learn the techno slang while we are at it.

Thus, after battling indecision for months, I joined the throng and bought an iPhone.

I uploaded my contacts, set my voice mail, and located the included GPS. I have not actually tried to navigate with it yet.

Side note: There are iPhone "gestures" one must master, and the terminology is strange and new to boomers. We are told to flick, drag, tap, double tap, stretch and pinch, and touch and drag.

I am working on these skills, but once I get my email account set up, Katy bar the door! For prior generations, this term is an American expression meaning get ready for trouble.

Could it be, however, that we are in love with these amazing gadgets because they seem magical, enchanted, mysterious, and thrilling. As Arthur C. Clarke once quipped, "Any sufficiently advanced technology is indistinguishable from magic."[23]

And certainly as we boomers age, we can be assured that we will never get lost when we take our daily walks using magical "advanced lifestyle tools" such as a GPS-equipped walker!

I don't want one of those, yet.

August 14, 2008

Waiting on the Cable Guy

"Fame means when your computer modem is broken,
the repair guy comes out to the house a little faster."

—SANDRA BULLOCK

Perhaps a little fame might have helped get the cable guy to our house quicker, but I doubt it.

The autodial instructions came days before the scheduled cable-internet technician's visit.

The company, whose name I shall not mention, called a second time via recorded message with a stern warning that I had better be there or else.

"Have someone over the age of eighteen present. Be sure the residence is open and accessible and put all pets away. The technician will call you twice on the day of service, and if you do not answer or miss the message, the service call will be cancelled."

And, you will die.

No, they did not say that, but they had my rapt attention. My instructions were to wait from 1:00 p.m. to 5:00 p.m.

At 3:00 p.m. I called the automated number. Here's a tip: Keep pushing zero until a live person answers. "He will be there in forty-five minutes," I was told. I called again at 4:00 p.m. and again at 5:10 p.m.

Actually, I was feeling pretty proud of myself for being so patient. By the way, the Encarta definition of patient, an adjective, is being able to endure waiting or delay without becoming annoyed or upset, or to persevere calmly when faced with difficulties.

I was indeed long-suffering and enduring that day, but enough is enough already.

"Where is he?" I screamed out loud at 5:30 p.m. to absolutely no one. Just one more call, I thought, and this time I will not be nice.

However, Murphy's Law was working overtime, and voice mail would not punch me through to a human being.

At 6:15 p.m. on a Monday night, the cable guy shows.

"Please tell me his name is not Larry the Cable Guy," I pleaded to the universe.

To make a long story short, after an exceedingly long time, the cable guy called for backup.

A second truck arrived. At 7:05 p.m., a third cable guy. This one knew what to do, and by 8:00 p.m. cable and internet were up and running.

"Do you guys really work this late past five o'clock?" I asked incredulously. I was properly impressed and grateful despite waiting all afternoon.

I just have a couple more questions for Larry, the first technician to arrive. Are all cable guys named Larry?

And, those guys with him, could they be his brother Daryl and his other brother Daryl (of *The Bob Newhart Show* fame)?

I wonder.

April 25, 2008

What Are You Waiting On, Friday?

*"When I am looking for an idea, I'll do anything
—clean the closet, mow the lawn, work in the garden."*

—KEVIN HENKES, author of *Chrysanthemum*

Writers are especially prone to "pushing the envelope." Often, we blame our procrastination on writer's block, a condition also known as "the midnight disease" because it afflicts writers about that time of night.

You don't have to be a writer to contract it, however. Last night, I got a bad case of it.

The midnight disease started for me a couple of hours before the stroke of midnight, leaving me blank with not a whisp of a story idea.

Have you heard about "drunk dials" or "drunk texts"? Probably, but have you ever heard of "writer's block panic calls"?

That's my affliction.

The worried calls to family and close friends start at the stroke of midnight: "It's almost the end of the week, and my column is due, again. Help! Any ideas?"

Such a call to my sister resulted in this reply: "Why do you always call at midnight? Can't you get writer's block a little earlier in the evening or a little earlier in the week?"

Apparently not, and according to Alice Flaherty in her book, *The Midnight Disease*, the author maintains that writer's block may be the result of brain activity being disrupted in the area of the brain that governs literary creativity.

I have no idea what interrupted my brain activity, but I did have one idea earlier in the week and wrote it down on a piece of paper, somewhere.

Actually, I write down everything I want to remember.

That way, instead of spending a lot of time trying to remember what it is I wrote down, I spend the time looking for the paper I wrote it down on.

I figure since I can't find that piece of paper and since I can't think of a thing to write, I might as well write about not having a thing to write.

My theory is that procrastinating is more than just avoiding tasks at hand. Perhaps we enjoy living on the edge because it feels deliciously like an elixir. We crave the rush of nearly crashing and burning, but being saved in the end.

Some of us put off buying airline tickets, hoping the price will get better; when in fact, it costs more by waiting.

Some shop madly on Christmas Eve because we say we love the spirit and excitement of last-minute gift buying only to find the stock "picked over" and no selection left.

What is it about putting projects off until Friday or the weekend or waiting until the last possible moment? We all do it.

Perhaps, we should not be so hard on ourselves either.

Personally, I live by the pun "only Robinson Crusoe had everything done by Friday."

And speaking of waiting on Friday, come to think of it, I think that was the idea I wrote on the lost piece of paper.

Now, I remember the story, too.

An old man waited for help on his rooftop surrounded by a flooding river. He asked his God for help and felt assured that assistance would come his way.

Soon, rescuers arrived in a small boat, but the man refused to join them. He explained that God would save him.

His situation worsened. Another rescue boat came and then another. Each time the old man said no, God would save him, and told the rescuers to go away.

He was expecting drama, the spectacle of miraculous intervention. Sadly, the man drowned as you might guess by now. The story continues that the stubborn old codger went straight to heaven where he wasted no time confronting his maker.

"Why didn't you save me?" the man demanded of God. "I believed you would."

"I tried three times," God said. "But you would not come. What were you waiting on, Friday?"

June 10, 2010

Siri, a High-Tech Genie in a Cell Phone, Not in a Bottle

"Master, master your wish is my command."[24]

—BARBARA EDEN,

in *I Dream of Jeannie*, television sitcom, 1964

These days, it seems that lots of people are wondering what to make of Siri, the new speech-recognition feature on the iPhone 4S. Have you heard of it yet?

Siri is a digital personal assistant that at times makes you believe it (she) could be human. It turns out that Siri is indeed a Scandinavian girl name meaning "Beautiful Victory," and thus, the name fits her perfectly.

Miss Siri is the source of plenty of discussion all right.

In fact, a standup comedian recently presented an interesting theory. He said Siri was actually "channeling" Barbara Eden who starred in the '60s television hit, *I Dream of Jeannie*.

He speculated that Siri was, in reality, a high-tech genie in a cell phone that could grant her master's every wish, just like the genie in the bottle did on the long-running NBC television series.

Interesting thought.

I do know for a fact that in 1964 when the series debuted, I never dreamed that one day I might have my own genie, too, just like Major Anthony Nelson. Remember him?

You may recall in the storyline that Major Nelson, played by Larry Hageman, was a top Apollo space program astronaut. He discovered his genie-in-a-bottle on a training mission when he went off course and landed on a remote, uncharted South Pacific island. There he found an odd bottle on the beach, uncorked it, and out popped a beautiful genie that coincidentally was named Jeannie.

Is it possible, I wonder, to have one's own personal assistant who, like Jeannie, is polite, humorous, quirky, and gets the job done on time?

I confess, I stood in line the first day with throngs of other Apple junkies hoping to find out.

Truth is, I wanted the 4S not so much because of its highly touted electronic personal assistant, Siri, but mostly because my old 3G could not keep up anymore. It moved too slowly struggling to open websites, among other problems, and it drove me crazy because the battery would not stay charged long.

I made the leap.

Now I am enjoying the luxury of having my own genie from whom I am learning all the ancient secrets of the universe. Might as well ask the genie-in-the-iPhone, right?

For example, "Siri, what is the meaning of life?"

To which she gave her standard reply, "I can't answer that now but give me some time to write a very long play in which nothing happens."[25] We are not exactly getting along famously yet. I am not altogether sure that Siri likes me. It's taking a while for us to get to know one another.

Curiously, she often misinterprets my questions and gets completely off track with her answers. Someone else can ask her the same questions, and her answers are spot on.

I am beginning to worry that she will never say with total and unconditional love, "Master, your wish is my command."

I am not alone, however. In a story in *USA Today*, the writer told Siri he loved her. Her answer: "Oh, stop."[26]

Major Nelson didn't have much better luck with his Jeannie. Here's an excerpt from one of the *I Dream of Jeannie* hit episodes:

Major Nelson: "Jeannie's turned against me."

Major Healey, Nelson's friend: "She can't turn against you. You're her master. She has to obey you."

Major Nelson: "Yeah, who says so?"

Major Healey: "I don't know, maybe it's in the genie manual."

Major Nelson: "Then how come she's deliberately disobeyed me?"

Major Healey: "Maybe she wasn't issued a genie manual."[27]

I don't think my Siri was issued a genie manual either. Nonetheless, I still absolutely love Siri.

If you are a Siri-hater, and they are out there, believe me, listen to what Richard Goodwin of knowyourmobile.com has to say: "While it may not be perfect, it is clear how much technology and innovation has gone into developing Siri . . . consider what technology can already do. Then imagine what it will be doing in five years, and that's when you'll see how exciting Siri's future really is."

So, I asked, "What does the future hold for you, Siri?"

Her reply, "I'm on it. What about a web search to answer your question? Here it is."[28] Whereupon, she provided on my iPhone screen a list of websites that give answers to the wonders and future of technology and what upgrades are next for Siri and for computers and other smart phones.

Looks like she must have read the genie manual after all, and I think she likes me now.

November 3, 2011

A Complicated Relationship with GPS

"You got to be careful if you don't know where you're going, because you might not get there."

—Yogi Berra

"If you think Missouri isn't beautiful, then you should take the drive Bonnie took me on last weekend," my friend Paige said.

Who is Bonnie, I wondered, thinking I've never heard Paige mention a "Bonnie"?

"She is my GPS," Paige answered and added that somehow Bonnie knew exactly what she needed that day—a peaceful and serene drive through the beautiful landscape of Missouri back roads.

"I was going from Kansas City to Jefferson City and Bonnie told me so confidently to turn off of I-70 onto Highway 87 and take that to Highway 179, that I did. It is as though she knew I needed my emotional batteries recharged with a picturesque drive in the country where I saw rolling hills, gorgeous flowering trees, green, green grass, cattle grazing in the valleys, and charming farmhouses and barns."

Paige continued, "How did she know that is exactly what I needed?" I think Paige meant that rhetorically, but I answered anyway.

"Well," I said, "she isn't Siri, so you couldn't ask her why, because of course one cannot have a two-way conversation with a GPS as one can with Siri."

We laughed, and Paige then explained more of her story, "Bonnie was patient, as though she was listening to me and intuitively taking me through a 'road less traveled.'

"Part way there," Paige said, "I stopped for coffee and water. She didn't like it as we know that no GPS wants us to veer off course or stop. I let her rant for a while because she probably needed to, and after all, she had not had a chance to say anything for a long time."

And thus, we have a perfect example of how we form relationships with our GPS, sometimes love and sometimes hate, or more likely annoyance and dependence.

It's the GPS racket that bothers my husband.

When we drive out west, we take a shortcut because we know it goes directly to my brother's house. Dominique, our GPS, does not know this and fusses at us incessantly with the familiar admonition, "recalculating, recalculating."

Finally, after enough of this noise, my husband will ask me to turn down the volume. She annoys him, but because of the love-hate relationship many of us have with our GPS, he also misses her reassuring voice and wants to be sure he is on the right road. Dominique will know. Then he asks me to turn up the volume.

I found an online story by Anna North about some interesting relationships people form with a GPS.

She writes, "More than one dude has fallen in love with the female voice on his GPS unit. She's so trustworthy, so calm, and reliable."[29]

North gives an example of such a case. Bruce Feiler of the *New York Times* wrote that he had "fallen for my GPS voice," and says he knows several guys who have developed a crush on the disembodied voice that tells them where to turn.[30] Wives and girlfriends might be lifting an eyebrow at that one as we speak.

Additionally, we know that couples often argue about whether to take the GPS lady's directions or not because she is not always accurate. I have met business travelers who say they would never leave home without her, knowing that she has saved them at the last minute when they were late for a meeting. However, she has also sent them down tangled dirt roads to the hinterlands.

Even though that soothing voice is almost human, we begin to wonder at times if my Dominique and Paige's Bonnie are simply ignorant, out of touch or behind the times.

Sometimes they simply cannot find the shortest, fastest route.

Goodness, it can be maddening.

Although we may love and hate our Global Positioning System and its voice, we must admit that these units, similar to any other technological device, are indispensable.

The problem is that the minute the devices leave the factory, the maps are outdated.

A business traveler's guide I found gives a solution: There is always the old-fashioned way if one is lost. Ask a local, and switch off your GPS, just so she knows who is boss.

But somehow, I don't think my Dominique would approve.

Think of it this way. If your GPS lady had a Facebook page, she would have to say on the profile page under "relationship"—it's complicated.

April 26, 2012

Telling a Story in Six Words

"It is with words as with sunbeams.
The more they are condensed, the deeper they burn."
—ROBERT SOUTHEY, English poet, 1774–1843

I was reading through an *AARP* magazine recently (and yes, I admit I am old enough to be a subscriber) when I discovered an article with an intriguing title, "Really Short Stories, in half a dozen words" by Larry Smith.

How can anyone write a story in six words, I wondered. Impossible, I decided.

Reading on, I learned that Ernest "Papa" Hemingway was once asked to do just that—tell a story in six words. As the story goes, Hemingway wrote, "For sale: baby shoes, never worn."

His powerful and fascinating story in just six words brings all sorts of possible scenarios immediately to mind. How did he choose exactly those six words, and how could we write our own six-word stories if we tried? Turns out, it is not so easy.

Give it a whirl yourselves; lots of folks have already tried. In fact, *AARP The Magazine* is currently challenging readers to do just that on its website.

Incidentally, six-word story telling started some time ago when *Smith Magazine* challenged readers to tell their life stories in six words. Harper Perennial later published favorite submissions in "Not Quite What I Was Planning: Six-Word Memoirs by Writers Famous & Obscure." Currently, websites such as sixwordmemoirs.com and smithmagazine.net are still encouraging readers to submit their own six-word life stories. Here are some of my favorites from *Smith Magazine* and *AARP The Magazine*:

Nearing 60, still on rough draft.[31]

I wear orange socks with red.[32]

Degree in programming, now I bake.[33]

Knocked on my door, never left.

What scares me, I'm considered above-average.

I still make coffee for two.

Sour grapes just need more sunshine.

Like it or not, I'm twittering.

There are tens of thousands of such six-word stories, and all leave me with searing questions as I try to imagine what the real-life story behind each of these is: "the joy, pathos, humor, or pain."

Although I know better and for one fleeting moment, I did indeed entertain the thought that writing six-word stories would be easy. But, as any writer knows, writing short is exceedingly difficult.

Stumped after a few attempts, I asked my third-grade grandson for help. Halen and I agreed that ten words, instead of six, would do just fine for our experiment. Without flinching and in a blink, he created these 10-worders:

"I like to shoot at hoops while watching flowers droop."

"Playing baseball rocks especially in your long-colored socks."

"I'd like to have a maid get my Gatorade!"

A word of warning: it takes time to write short, lots of time, unless you are a third-grader.

To write concisely, as Thomas Jefferson once said, "is the most valuable of all talents."

And William Shakespeare, in *Hamlet*, was the master of succinctness when he penned this famous six-worder, "Brevity is the soul of wit!"

To which I add, "So, I'll sign my name and quit." But wait, that was seven words. I'll try again. "Six worders, no piece of cake!"

Ta-da!

July 16, 2009

Attack of the Zombie (Email Spam)
Part 1

"I do not fear computers. I fear lack of them."

—Isaac Asimov

If a zombie attacks your email account, as one did to mine recently, don't despair and don't give up on computers.

I look at it as an adventure in living my own personal bad B-movie about zombies, scary but funny.

The first step is to act fast, change your password, and be glad you have email friends who will let you know right away that your account has been spammed.

Incidentally, I am not speaking of canned meat made largely from pork when I speak of spam. No, I am talking about unwanted emails sent out in bulk purportedly from one's own personal email address.

The attack of the zombie.

James Clark, who writes for Yahoo's contributor network, explains a zombie email attack: "They are called zombie because they stay dormant until activated by a signal over an internet connection. Once activated they use your computer to send out junk email. They try to collect credit card information or other private data by 'phishing.'"

Some of these attacks are true viruses that send their tentacles deep into your system.

Other attacks, such as what happened to me, are not viruses at all and work through an email server to steal one's email address book. When I researched email zombies, I found that they often attack free accounts such as Yahoo, Gmail, Hot Mail, GMX, Zoho, AIM, GMX, and a host of others.

That is exactly what happened to my free email account almost two weeks ago.

It was not pretty, but I corrected it in less than an hour after I received a 5:30 a.m. phone call from a friend alerting me to the "phishing" email she received, supposedly from me.

However, the repercussions of this action lasted for days, although I am happy to report that all is well for now in my cyberworld.

That is, until it happens again.

Experts say that if you have an email account, any email account, it is only a matter of "when," not "if" this will happen to you.

Do not panic, there is life after a zombie attack, but you may need to seek professional help right away.

"Computer viruses are a lot like children—the longer they're left alone, the more trouble they can get into," says Julie Marto, "Computer Mom" in the *Medfield Press*. "It's like leaving your sixteen-year-old home alone," she adds. "One overnight is okay but left alone for a week, there's going to be a mess."[34]

Marto is a stay-at-home mom who started a computer business in her home to train customers in software proficiency. Today, her business has changed so much that nearly all she does is virus cleanup, and she does that within twenty-four hours of an attack if at all possible.

Removing viruses and other bugs from computers has become a big business indeed.

Even bigger is the business of the spammers themselves. Spamming is now a gigantic operation, the business of organized cyber-crime.

Dear readers, please erase your visual images of spammers right now. Those no longer apply. You know what you are thinking—the mental picture of a nerdy teen spammer or a forty-year-old guy who sits in his underwear drinking beer in his parents' basement.

At first, when one's email is spammed, one wants to track the perpetrator down immediately and turn him or her over to the proper authorities. Not likely and not possible.

One is fighting, instead, a giant Internet Zombie network, not a crazed spammer in someone's basement.

When I researched Internet Zombie networks, I found that they are sometimes referred to as "botnets," a collection of software robots that run by themselves and automatically.

However, there are most certainly people at the helm of these anonymous underground networks. They are called "bot herders," who rent the services of the botnet out to third parties to send out spam attack messages and requests for credit card information.

Does this seem confusing? It is, but I learned how to understand it, somewhat, and to survive it, for the time being. Keep in mind, however, that here are no ironclad do's and don'ts to follow.

Next week in Part II, I will tell you about my harrowing but funny experience with Zombies, botnets, bot herders, and phishermen—my own real-life, bad B-movie.

I am just hoping it does not turn out to be the sequel, *Return of the Zombie*.

January 27, 2011

Attack of the Zombie (Email Spam)
Part 2

---

*"How is it that one match can start a forest fire,
but it takes a whole box of matches to start a campfire?"*

—CHRISTY WHITEHEAD

When perpetrators of cyber-crime spammed my email account recently, it only took a single action, one match if you will, to start a forest fire of chain reactions.

A whole box of matches could not set afire what followed.

I wrote about this last week and promised to tell you "the rest of the story," as the late Paul Harvey used to say.

After a 5:30 a.m. call alerting me to the "attack of the zombie" on my free email account, my day was no longer mine. And oh joy, the fun continued for nine more days.

I felt like I was stomping out wildfires across Kansas with my bare feet.

If you have not heard about "zombie" email attacks before, here is what they do.

Zombies visit you via an email you received and then lie dormant until activated by a signal over an internet connection. Zombies use your computer to send out junk email, usually in an attempt to collect credit card information or other personal data. The practice is called "phishing."

Apparently, the email from "me," perpetrated by the zombie, went far and wide.

Its message indicated something like this: "I am stranded in the UK in London and someone stole my purse. I lost all my credit cards and money and my passport, and I can't get home. Please email me a credit card number so I can get the money to get back home. Thanks, Kay."

It was still early in the morning when all phones in the house began to ring at the same time, including the landline, my business cell phone, my personal cell phone, and my husband's cell phone.

My email box filled with messages from concerned friends, family, and business associates.

Text messages came in bunches; someone knocked on my front door to alert me to the email problem; and others tracked my husband down at work. Friends posted on Facebook and tweeted me.

By 9:00 a.m., I was in full combat mode fighting the attack of the zombie.

After checking with my computer guru friends, I learned that my "mother ship" computer and laptop were most likely just fine. Virus checks turned up nothing. I changed all my passwords on all my email accounts. All was well in my cyberworld.

I thought I was finished stomping out brush fires set by the cyber criminals.

But the phone calls continued, "Kay, I think you gave me a virus just now, did you know that?"

"It's not a virus," I tried to explain. And so my day continued.

My husband called to tell me he had concerned folks in his office asking the same question. Most people wanted to know if I was OK and if I really needed money, but one wondered why I didn't call my husband if I was indeed stranded in London. One asked why the American Embassy didn't help me.

The Examiner emailed to tell me readers stopped by to alert them to the crime.

The claims adjuster who handled our homeowner's insurance claim last year called from the home office because he received the email from me as well.

Exasperated, I took a break from all this and went to lunch with the neighbor gals.

While we were eating, the waitress came to one of my friends and said she had a phone call. Puzzled, she went to the kitchen to take the call on their restaurant phone. It was her husband, who heard from another neighbor who was worried if I was OK. "No, she is fine," she said, "Kay is sitting across the table from me eating a burrito, and I can assure you she is not in London."

As the next nine days unfolded, I heard from old college friends and high school classmates, parents of teams, clubs, and organizations I was involved with when our kids were in school, former neighbors who now live out of state, and someone we sold a car to who now lives in Florida.

The good news in all this is the fact that I have both real life and cyber friends who have my back. That's nice to know.

Thank you, dear readers and friends, and I sincerely hope you do not encounter a zombie as I did.

Do's and don'ts are simple—change your password regularly on email accounts, especially free ones, monitor your account regularly, and don't worry too much about this happening to you. If it does, fix it and go on. These days, it is a fact of life in cyberworld.

There is one more loose end I have not taken care of yet, and I better get on it right away, come to think of it.

When I walked into the beauty shop last week, I was met with this comment from my beautician, "Kay, you better call the police and let them know you are back safe and sound from London."

"Why would I need to call them?" I asked. My beautician's reply came back quickly, accompanied by a sheepish look, "Oh, some of us turned you in."

February 3, 2011

Tweeting with Charlie Sheen,
the #Sheenious

I have a confession.

Quite recently, for reasons that escape me, I succumbed to the hot, trending, global madness of tweeting with Charlie Sheen.

I joined the ranks of 3,569,518 followers of Charlie Sheen, the number of followers at the time I joined. However, that total grows exponentially.

For a while I resisted, but eventually the #sheenious won me over, #Duh,winning.

Perhaps, @Mozarkite (moi) joined out of curiosity, I don't know. One thing is for certain, Sheen's tweets are entertaining, edgy, and never boring.

By Twitter standards, Sheen has tweeted, as of this writing, a measly 203 times, peanuts in the Twitter world.

He follows only forty-two people as of this writing, and I am not among them.

Twitter tells me that I know eight people who also follow Charlie Sheen. However, I am not exactly sure why I know @lostremote or @ShakespeareGeek, but never mind that.

The point is, no one can keep up with Charlie Sheen's shenanigans, let alone his number of followers.

It's mind boggling. No, it's madness.

In fact, just about everything about Charlie Sheen is maddening, even fun, and at the very least surprising.

Thus, imagine my surprise when I clicked on the @charliesheen button and found that we do in fact follow one person in common: @FloydMayweather.

Problem is I don't know who Floyd Mayweather is, and why I follow him. When did I do that, I wonder.

Naturally, I immediately searched the web and found out that he is ranked as, #Duh,winning, the number one Welterweight boxer by many boxing publications. Yes, he is indeed the number one pound-for-pound best boxer in the world.

And I don't know him, but we both follow the #sheenious. It is fair for you to wonder, when will this madness end?

I wonder that, too, but the answer is not anytime soon.

A Time.com blog notes that "Charlie Sheen, not merely content with taking up more news cycle time than could ever be deemed necessary, is now seeking to trademark twenty-two of his catchphrases. Don't we all have enough to be getting on with for Sheen to be concerned with this? And how the heck did he get to twenty-two without us noticing?"[35]

Sheen is already selling T-shirts and other merchandise highlighting some of his trending catchphrases that are making their way into the English language, whether we like it or not.

A reporter for PCmag.com writes, "Whether you think actor Charlie Sheen's recent behavior is . . . sad, highly entertaining, or hilarious, one thing is for sure—he has made quite the impression on the Twitterverse."[36] In "Twitterverse" these phrases are preceded by a hashtag symbol (#). If you use a hashtag before a word it shows those tweets more easily in a Twitter search and also shows you similar tweets on the same topic.

When a hashtag word becomes popular, it often is listed on Twitter as a Trending Topic.

And thus, many people now use in their common vernacular #winning and #Duh,winning to generally express something you've done that might be considered winning.

#TigerBlood—if you have something to tweet that requires the extra punch.

And #Buh-Bye—when you need to end a conversation.

One more thing before I say #Buh-Bye. Miley Cyrus rejoined Twitter this week after a year-and-a-half absence. Here is why, according to a tweet from Miley Cyrus herself: "I'm not gonna lie. I came back to Twitter for two reasons: My fans and to follow @charliesheen #winning."[37]

#TigerBlood.

April 14, 2011

Novels Written with Flying Thumbs
on Cell Phones—Best Sellers!

"I'm so far behind, I think I'm first."

—ANONYMOUS quote on a cutout wooden
plaque of a turtle, on my kitchen counter

Just when I thought I was current, if not ahead, on all forms of electronic communication, I find out that I am woefully behind. I just learned about a new genre of writing—cell phone storytelling.

Yes, mostly young authors, but some as old as forty, are writing novels on their mobile phone and using flying dexterous thumbs that defy understanding.

Granted, this is happening primarily in Japan, where I read that cell phone novelists and most citizens prefer writing on their phones to typing on computers. Still, the idea is making its way to the US.

As preposterous as the notion first sounded to me, I am grasping the concept better since learning that half of Japan's best-selling novels began as cell phone novels, uploaded to web sites, and later published as hard or soft-cover books.

A famous literary journal in Japan asked if this new genre could kill traditional authors and writing as we know it.

Apparently not, as Shigeru Matsushima, an editor at Starts Publishing, writes, "It's not that the young cell phone novelist has a desire to write and that the cell phone happened to be there . . . Instead, in the course of exchanging e-mail, this tool called the cell phone instilled in them a desire to write."[38]

An article in the *New York Times*, "Thumbs Race as Japan's Best Sellers Go Cellular," concludes that, "Indeed, many cell phone novelists had never written fiction before, and many of their readers had never read novels before, according to publishers."[39]

So instilling the love of reading and writing works for me. More power to them, I say.

The *New York Times* article adds this bonus for cell phone story-tellers: "Whatever their literary talents, cell phone novelists are racking up the kind of sales that most more experienced, traditional novelists can only dream of."[40]

One young woman by the pen name Rin, was voted No. 1 in Japan with her text novel, a story of tragic love between childhood friends. After uploading to a web site where readers could follow as she wrote, the novel was turned into a 142-page hardcover book that sold over 400,000 copies.

That sells me on the idea.

I am starting mine now, but I am not quite as fast as the kid writers, since there is the not-so-small matter of arthritis and carpal tunnel that only complicate things.

Incidentally, I forgot to mention that cell phone novelists use texting abbreviations, emoticons, and text smiles to tell their story, as well as leaving out flowery descriptions. Plot happens fast and characters never fully develop. I think this genre could be losing me and probably anyone over the age of twelve as well.

Take a look at this sample of the beginning of one of these texting novels to understand my point:

"Brk Tskot rOd her mAr BlAz a+ the prayri n surch of wht she new she wud fnd. Hrsh elements & Mac, the lst pursn on urth she wantd 2 see this AM."

Translation: Brook Tescott rode her mare Blaze across the prairie in search of what she knew she would find—harsh elements and Mac (Chad McPherson), the last person on earth she wanted to see this morning.

I will let you know how my first cell phone novel is going. I may be too old for this. TTYL.

March 25, 2010

Key to Creativity—Ask a Kid or a Senior

*"All children are artists. The problem is
how to remain an artist once he grows up."*

—PABLO PICASSO

Are you searching for ways to be more imaginative and creative and make life simpler?

If so, I would suggest this: Ask a kid or a senior.

Here's why. Kids and seniors know the secret of creativity.

For everyone else somewhere between childhood and the September of life, creativity often appears to take a vacation.

Nonetheless, we can be creative whenever we want, can't we? In fact, we are all Michelangelo's at heart, if we could just figure out how to remain creative.

I like the following definition of creativity from Charles Mingus, an American musician, who said, "Creativity is more than just being different. Anybody can plan weird; that's easy. What's hard is to be as simple as Bach. Making the simple, awesomely simple, that's creativity."

Therefore, creativity equals simplicity. That's hard to do when we are in the "busy" years of our lives.

In our childhood years, we knew how to make complex things simple, awesomely simple, as Charles Mingus noted. However, life happened in between and our imagination went on hiatus, meaning a long break.

We wish it stayed with us, but it didn't.

Instead, our creativity became what McDonald's founder Ray Kroc once observed, "Creativity is a highfalutin word for the work I have to do between now and Tuesday."

There was no time or energy to be creative.

Then, faster than a speeding bullet the "senior" years arrive, although we may no longer feel like Superman or Superwoman. There is good news, however, because those years come with a bonus.

Creativity returns and leads seniors to dreams they left behind as children.

Aha, the very same reason dessert is served last. It's the best part.

Casey Mase wrote a story for the blog *Live Now* in which she explored the possibility that creativity does indeed increase with age.

She asks each of us to remember the "creative types" we encountered in our youth. You remember, the ones who never cared what others thought and seemed to have the gift of free self-expression.

Turns out a recent *Psychology Today* article presents the theory that people over the age of sixty-five are exuding characteristics of creative artists, those same creative free spirits of our youth.

Yes, they mean those kids we remember from high school who ignored social expectations and did whatever they pleased.

Artist Louise Nevelson commented that she never feels age, and that if you have creative work, you don't age.

Perhaps that is why so many over the age of sixty excel at creative pursuits and find great joy in them, such as oil painting, pastels, carpentry, gardening, jewelry making, music, poetry, woodworking, or writing.

Relaxation sets in, boundaries disappear and creativity returns.

In Casey Mase's blog, she explains more of this *Psychology Today* premise, "The area of the brain involved in self-conscious awareness and censoring, the prefrontal cortex, is thinner in the aging brain. In a population of older adults, this may account for their reduced need for acceptance and an ambition to speak their minds—common traits among artists."

Thus, the brains of creative artists and the aging could be similar.

Casey's blog poses the question, "Could the September of your life be the best time to pursue the creative dreams of your youth? And the converse of that: If in our youth we had let go of our stresses, self-censorship, and self-consciousness, could we have been the creative souls we wanted to be?"

Since kids know a lot, I asked Grandson Cole, age eight, what he thought.

He showed me his Dude Diary, in which all the answers of the universe are stored.

The diary asked, "Dude, what's on your mind? What are you thinking about, man?"

Cole wrote, "Pretty much, I just want to draw a nice cat and dog." And that, dear readers, is simplicity and creativity at its best.

August 18, 2011

Summers Past

"I said they could join us. They're baby boomers."

Homegrown Tomatoes
Sound Better Than Ever

We were driving from Colorado back to Missouri this past week when we began to notice signs on all restaurant doors that there would be no tomatoes served inside their establishments, temporarily that is.

Now I get it. That is why my BLT sandwich was minus the T when we stopped for lunch at a turnpike rest stop.

This sudden dearth of tomatoes, due to fears of salmonella contamination, makes me nostalgic for homegrown tomatoes and summers past. In those days, we had never heard of salmonella. We simply picked luscious tomatoes grown in our backyards, washed off the garden dirt, and enjoyed.

It was a simpler time. Can we go back?

I miss those homegrown grilled tomatoes, stuffed tomatoes, canned stewed tomatoes, green tomato relish, tomato salsa, tomato sauce, and my favorite—barbecue sauce made with tomato paste, vinegar, and sugar.

As Lewis Grizzard quipped, "It's difficult to think anything but pleasant thoughts while eating a homegrown tomato."

Oh, those were the days.

Since I am waxing nostalgic about summers past and tomatoes, here are a few more thoughts about tomatoes for you to ponder with me. Grandma said in order to grow great tomatoes, plant them in full sun where they can get direct sunlight for most of the day.

Plant in well-drained soil away from roots and grass in late March, but only on an overcast, cool day.

If you plant on a sunny day, make a tent from newspapers to protect the tender, young plants for a week or so. Cage them at first and stake later.

Mulch is a good idea, and one must keep an eye out for pests.

Hopefully, if all goes well, you can pick in June when they are pink, not deep red. Sit them on your counter top and let them ripen at their own speed. Do not refrigerate until they are fully ripe.

If you missed the March planting time as I did, you can still plant patio container tomatoes and have them by August.

June 12, 2008

Fried Chicken Has to Start Somewhere

Every newspaper has its own colorful humorist, but none can compare in my way of thinking with the *Kansas City Star's* late Bill Vaughan.

Once, while talking about the good old days, Vaughan quipped, "A convenience food today is one that is already cooked. In grandmother's time, it was a chicken she didn't have to kill personally."

Young readers may not understand and cover their ears for the rest of this story.

Those of us who grew up in the '50s, especially those on a farm, know exactly what Bill Vaughan meant and will remember the summer ritual known as "dressing chickens."

Or, I should I say, killing chickens we knew personally.

If you did not grow up on a farm, you may have missed this practice, but if you did, you know exactly what I mean.

In those days, my grandmother was the chief chicken dresser (a polite term for chicken killer).

Here is how this ceremonial chore unfolded.

When chicken-butchering time arrived, my grandmother, mother, and all relatives within shouting distance marched resolutely to the chicken house.

Grandma set up a cauldron of boiling water in the yard. My mother's job was to catch the squawking chickens, hold them upside down by the legs, and hand them over to my grandmother.

Grandma would twist the chicken's neck with a quick pop so that the chicken could not feel any pain. She would then lay it on the ground, and step on its neck with her boot. Then, she would pull the head off and let the chicken flop around headless, squirting blood everywhere.

It was a comical sight because sometimes the chicken would get up and walk, minus the head of course.

After the required amount of time passed, the women took turns picking up the flopping chickens holding them by their feet and dipping the bodies into the caldron's scalding water.

My grandmother and mother seemed to know exactly how long was long enough. At the perfect moment, they would hand off the wet, smelly chickens to us kids to pluck.

Incidentally, one can never forget the smell of a wet chicken.

With eyes wide open in astonishment, we kids took the wet chickens in one hand and began plucking the feathers with the other. That was our job.

We did not complain, because for the next two weeks we feasted on fried chicken and all the trimmings. That was our payoff.

Mashed potatoes covered with salt and pepper and white chicken gravy, homemade rolls with real butter, green beans from the garden cooked with bacon grease and onions, corn on the cob slathered with butter, homegrown tomatoes, and strawberry shortcake, a flat shortbread served with thick cream direct from the cow and strawberries straight from the patch.

I make no judgment about the way we ate in those days except to say this: I can still smell and taste that glorious food. We ate the same fare every day at noon dinner and again at supper for two solid weeks while the chickens were fresh. (Note of explanation to the younger crowd—no one had a deep freezer.)

And, we never tired of eating fried chicken because, after all, it was chicken "dressing" time.

June 19, 2008

Laziness is a Virtue in the Summertime

"Being a child at home in the summer is a high-risk occupation. If you call your mother at work thirteen times an hour, she can hurt you."

—ERMA BOMBECK

Parents, if the kiddos are driving you crazy this summer, try this.

Have them do absolutely nothing—as long as it is outside, that is!

If they are bored already with video games and television, here is an idea—let us go back to the "lazy, hazy, crazy days of summer."

A time when laziness was a virtue and children and parents alike did as little as possible.

Maybe it was too hot in those days to do anything productive because few of us had air conditioning. Staying outside to find a cool breeze and shade was vital. So, if one was outside already, one might as well play.

Incidentally, none of our summer fun cost a penny.

An imagination was the only thing one needed in order to find unending summer fun.

Mostly, we did nothing at all except daydream and get really, really dirty.

We created elaborate roads and bridges in the dirt for our toy cars, hunted lightning bugs, and played hide and seek in the woods until someone gave up or got hurt.

And yes, kids did eat mud pies. The mud pies, by the way, were constructed with small sticks and stones to glue the substance together. Occasionally, we older ones might feed the younger kids a mud pie just to see if they would eat it, and sometimes they would try.

Our playhouse was a nasty old chicken house, but in our eyes, a mansion. This child's version of a remodeling project took days, until eventually the "secret" playhouse was ready for old furniture and broken dishes from the shed. We thought our parents never knew. Looking back, I can only imagine the chicken droppings and disgusting grime on that dirt floor.

We spent hours throwing sticks to the dog, often following him into tall grass and woods where we contracted "stick-tights," chigger bites, ticks, poison ivy, and nettle stings. However, even pests and noxious weeds did not stop our forays.

And it would not be a perfect summer afternoon without spitting watermelon seeds from the porch or lying on one's back on the ground to search for shapes in the clouds. In the evening, the entire family would admire the night beauty of the stars once again from the porch, and if we were lucky, talk Dad into taking us to town for an ice cream cone.

Once again, I sigh wistfully and ask, "Can we go back?"

Of course we cannot, but we can try on for size the idea of summer laziness. I guarantee you will love it and so will the kiddos!

As writer Sam Keen quipped, "Deep summer is when laziness finds respectability."

June 26, 2008

You Gotta Love the Patriotism
of Bygone Days

"You have to love a nation that celebrates its independence every July 4, not with a parade of guns, tanks, and soldiers who file by the White House in a show of strength and muscle, but with family picnics where kids throw Frisbees, the potato salad gets iffy, and the flies die from happiness. You may think you have overeaten, but it is patriotism."

—ERMA BOMBECK

Ah yes, I remember that "iffy" potato salad and the flies, too, at many a Fourth of July celebration of my youth.

Surprisingly, what I remember most besides the fireworks is a television monologue given by the late great Red Skelton in celebration of Independence Day. Skelton was a comedian who rose to stardom between the '50s and '70s, delighting audiences coast-to-coast with his weekly television show.

After all these years, I remember very little about Red Skelton's then famous "Pledge of Allegiance" monologue. I just remember that I loved it at the time.

Naturally, I had to do a bit of research to find the details. I hope you enjoy remembering it as well, or if it is the first time you have heard it, you may want to watch the video.

Either way, I recommend searching on the internet for the YouTube video of Red Skelton's "Pledge of Allegiance" first performed in 1969.

You will not soon forget it.

Skelton tells a story about how his teacher Mr. Laswell of Harrison School in Vincennes, Indiana, felt his students had come to think of the Pledge of Allegiance as merely something to recite in class each day, something monotonous.

Mr. Laswell remarked to the students, "If I may, may I recite it and try to explain to you the meaning of each word?"

He continued, "I—meaning me, an individual, a committee of one.

"Pledge—dedicate all of my worldly goods to give without self-pity. Allegiance—my love and my devotion.

"To the flag—our standard, Old Glory, a symbol of freedom. Wherever she waves, there's respect because your loyalty has given her a dignity that shouts freedom is everybody's job!

"The United—that means we have all come together.

"States of America—individual communities that have united into forty-eight (now fifty) great states; individual communities with pride and dignity and purpose; all divided with imaginary boundaries, yet united to a common purpose, and that is love for country.

"And to the republic—a state in which sovereign power is invested in representatives chosen by the people to govern. And government is the people and it is from the people to the leaders, not from the leaders to the people."

Red Skelton's entire rendition of Mr. Laswell's speech is too long for this column.

However, I will share with you here his final admonition to his students, "We are one nation so blessed by God that we are incapable of being divided, which means, boys and girls, it is as much your country as it is mine."[42]

You gotta love it!

July 3, 2008

Summer Romances
Rarely Survived Until September

"What the heart has once owned and had, it shall never lose."

—HENRY WARD BEECHER

Summer romances, a cultural phenomenon, were big in the '50s and '60s.

I doubt if teens today truly understand what our summer romances were like—the giddiness, the misery, the sweetness, the inevitable parting.

Teen sweethearts do not part these days at summer's end. They simply text each other into infinity and blog unceasingly on Facebook.

We had one option and one only—write letters or hope they came.

Usually, we never saw or talked to our summer loves again. For me, summer love meant Frank, and yes, Pete, too.

I met Frank one summer at swim camp, and the next summer I met Pete while working out-of-state at a summer resort.

Both relationships lasted only for the summers in question. Letters were the way we stayed in touch at summer's end, as few people in those days had the technology to make long-distance phone calls. Traveling was out of the picture as well.

Eventually and predictably, in the fall, the letters slowed and the romances faded.

When love went bad, girls and guys alike cried in our cherry phosphates while losing ourselves in movie and song.

It was a bittersweet, delicious time of life.

Once, years later, just out of curiosity, I tried to find each of these dreamy guys.

I learned that Frank pursued a calling as a chaplain and likely died in Vietnam. Pete pursued a career as a hippie and might still be in Haight-Ashbury.

So, life works out.

Yet, I still remember the songs about the heartbreak of summer when romances were sure to be fleeting and nearly always heartbreaking.

"Summer Nights" from the blockbuster movie *Grease*. John Travolta and Olivia Newton-John sang "Summer Nights" about their rockin' summer romance of 1959.

The lyrics of "See You in September" by The Happenings sounded like it was directed at lonely kids away from home for the summer.

While at summer camp, we teens often met our true love only to realize too late that our storybook romance would be short-lived. Or, we would worry if the boyfriend or girlfriend back home would wait for us and vice versa.

Gary Lewis and The Playboys sang the hit song, "Save Your Heart For Me."

Chad and Jeremy's ballad "A Summer Song" admonished summer lovers to live in the moment because autumn would surely come.

The Beach Boys sang the upbeat "All Summer Long," while Brian Hyland crooned "Sealed with a Kiss" as he wrote letters to his sweetheart lest she forget him.

Do kids today have any idea what a summer romance was really like in the summers of our youth? Romantic. Unrequited. Unconsummated. I am guessing no.

At least we had the comfort of knowing that summer romance could live on in our hearts forever.

July 10, 2008

Making Hay While the Sun Shines
Was Once Serious Business

In recalling summers past, one would be remiss not to include the practice of "making hay" that took on huge, community-like proportions in the month of July.

At the risk of sounding antediluvian (old-fashioned, antiquated, or as in one who lived before the Biblical flood), I feel compelled to explain "putting up" or "making hay" for those too young to know the terminology.

Haying was a vital, communal, and social event in the '50s and '60s.

The world stopped when it was time to "make hay."

Incidentally, you can't "make hay" when it is raining. Grass must be cut and left to dry in the sun because it is next to impossible to cut wet grass, and if you bale the dry grass when it is raining, the hay will rot. Farmers would try to cut the grass when it was likely that the sun would shine all day and continue shining for a couple of days more.

Timing is everything because baling hay is a race against Mother Nature.

Mowing too soon right before a big rain can ruin the crop. Typically, the hay is baled in midday when the sun is blazing.

Thus, the term "Make hay while the sun shines."

Putting up hay (meaning putting hay in the barn) required long days and grueling work under the blistering sun.

Dinner was before noon so that crews could get started when the sun was its hottest.

Women and children always ate after the men, no exceptions. Heavy dinners of fried chicken or steak, potatoes and gravy, home-made rolls, and pie or cake were the typical fare. Iced-tea, sweetened with what seemed like five pounds of sugar, was dipped from a five-gallon bucket. Farmers shared equipment, tractors, and wagons.

They worked each other's fields and no money was exchanged. Only the boys on the crew were paid.

Joining a hay crew became a quick lesson in life for them, too.

The young guys were offered a choice of pay, $1.25 per hour, or $0.02 per bale. Since two cents per bale did not sound like much, novices often opted for the hourly wage, but they only did that once.

In four hours, a crew could load 1,000 bales and earned $5.00 if paid hourly.

If they opted for the two cents per bale, they would make $20.00.

Doing the math, it figures that if a small crew put up 1,000 bales a day with each bale weighing fifty pounds, they would be lifting nearly fifty tons a day since they had to lift each bale twice, once on the wagon and once in the barn.

It was good exercise and good money in those days.

But by the mid-'70s, farmers could not find enough young men to work the hay crews, so they began opting for new technology, balers that produced the big round bales one sees in fields today.

Farmers could manage the baler alone, effectively ending the need for hay crews and the community of people it took to put up hay.

So, when our kids hear, "You had better make hay while the sun shines," they rightly assume "act while conditions are favorable."

We baby boomers, however, could be remembering this instead—better get that hay put up before it rains.

It was another time.

July 17, 2008

Summer's End Brought Road Trips and Slide Shows

August was vacation month for those who grew up in the '50s and '60s.

When July ended, it was time to pack as much as one could into the station wagon, whatever the make (ours was a DeSoto), and take a road trip.

The clock was ticking because the lazy, carefree summer now had an end in sight. School would start in mere weeks.

Looking back, I have to wonder who was left to "mind the store" since it seemed as though everyone was on vacation in August.

And oh my, the things we took on vacation.

A neighbor once reminded us as we prepared for a trip, "Those who say you can't take it with you never saw your car packed for a vacation trip."

For example, the shoebox.

All our shoes were tossed into a large cardboard box and put in the back of the wagon next to the smaller box of Spam and white bread, a necessity for roadside lunch stops.

Once we made it all the way from northwest Missouri to Falls City, Nebraska, before we realized that our shoebox was still at home. We turned around and went back for it.

I also remember spending entire road trips playing in the back of our green DeSoto station wagon, sans seat belts of course. We had not heard of those yet.

One cross-country trip in our "woody" station wagon included a full load of travelers, including parents, we three siblings, our grandmother, and aunt. The trip was quite similar to the movie *Vacation,* although no one died en route. And that is all I will say about that.

When seeing "sights," self-respecting travelers took pictures, typically in the form of slides. Lots of slides.

If you were up-to-date like our dad, you would have a screen and a fancy projector with slide boxes so that the slides could be fed in quickly one after the other. The only problem was that most folks had boxes and boxes of slides.

It was expected that you would call friends and family together after the trip and show slides. Everyone did this. We watched each other's slide shows and no one complained.

Can you imagine how boring we would find that today?

The vacation slides often depicted shots posed by historical roadside markers. Trust me, there were hundreds of them between Missouri and the Pacific Ocean.

Some slides featured well-known landscape scenes in national parks, and others focused on visits with relatives. Nothing creative, just expected and predictable photos.

We didn't care.

We watched and watched, never tiring of them, and then ate cake and ice cream afterwards.

I once heard someone describe a vacation and its subsequent slide show as just like love. We anticipate it with pleasure, experience it with discomfort, and remember it with nostalgia.

And that we did quite happily.

July 24, 2008

Paint by Number Crafts
Filled Our Summer Hours

"At moments of great enthusiasm it seems to me that no one in the world has ever made something this beautiful and important."

—M.C. Escher

Paint by number kits were the rage in the '50s and '60s before they slipped out of favor and out of sight.

Critics said the kits were not creative and exceedingly ugly. Even a horse painting? Surely not. I thought mine was beautiful.

Never once did I think my painting ugly, especially my prized "Horse in the Meadow" masterpiece.

Nevertheless, the fad soon died, despite the fact that parents kept kids out of mischief by giving them paint by number projects to fill the idle summer hours.

It worked like magic, too. As soon as we finished one canvas, we wanted another.

I, for one, burst with pride at my painting of a horse grazing in a field. Previously, I had displayed absolutely no artistic talent whatsoever, but now I could paint a horse! Who knew? Hey, the finished canvas looked like a real painting to me at age eight.

Remember the most popular paint by number kits of the era? They were the horses, of course, as well as the dogs, mountains, lighthouses, and perhaps the most painted picture of all, the "Last Supper."

Want to try to paint by number again? You can because this once-popular craft is back.

Collectable kits or new styles are available at craft and toy stores, including online stores. These kits are among the most popular arts and crafts kits sold today.

I can guess why.

The simplicity of painting without having to think certainly appeals to most of us as a way to slow our harried, fast-paced days.

It is meditative, calming, and restorative. It takes us back to a simpler time. Do not laugh; it works!

Painting by number calms one down while one concentrates. For example, brushing the burnt sienna paint (reddish brown) in the number five spot on the horse's back. It is rather difficult to think or worry about anything else when painting the required color.

Perhaps that is why when I visit my ninety-year-old mother I note that she and her friends in the care center are blissfully content when they paint by number.

Granted, their attention spans may not be long and some may need assistance, but all in all, they find joy in producing their very own artistic works simply by following the numbers.

Sky blue is their number one favorite color. A grassy green is number two, and sunny yellow is three.

Oh, if life were only that simple at any age, eight or ninety.

I wonder where I put that horse picture, now that I think about it.

July 31, 2008

Cherished Summers Are
at the End of the Rainbow

"Summer ends, and Autumn comes,
and he who would have it otherwise would have
high tides always and a full moon every night."

—HAL BORLAND

Summer is waning. We never see the end coming, do we, and its end always breaks my heart.

I planned to have a lazy, carefree summer with lots of time to swim, picnic, and read, just like I did in the summers of my youth.

Instead, I painted the deck, attended meetings, fought broadleaf weeds in the yard, and visited relatives.

Each year I continue to search for this "end of the rainbow," if you will, a futile attempt to recapture the untroubled and happy-go-lucky days of summers past.

Incidentally, if you have ever walked toward the end of a rainbow you know that it will continue to move further away. In truth, a rainbow does not actually exist in a particular location, just like cherished summer memories.

In this series about a time before air conditioning, we have revisited a variety of summer memories.

We talked about enjoying homegrown tomatoes, dressing chickens, championing summer laziness as a virtue, loving the patriotism of bygone days, reminiscing about long, lost summer romances, "putting up hay," taking road trips and watching each other's slide shows, and spending hours of our summer vacation doing crafts such as paint by number kits.

And there are more lovely memories to recall as well. Memories such as these:

Playing outside all day with no sunscreen or bug spray for protection as we wandered through the timber naming the trees and rocks in order to reenact our favorite western movies.

"Meet you at Twin Oaks," I said to my siblings and cousins. "I will be at Lone Rock watching out for outlaws." We believed we were a posse of cowboys, lawmen, and cowgirls chasing the bad guys.

We stayed out all morning in this pursuit until my mother honked the car horn to call us home for dinner, served at noon straight up. She never knew where we were, but assumed we would come back if injured too badly.

I remember riding a Go-Kart made from scraps of metal and an old gas engine, and driving it very fast while releasing the governor so it would move even faster, often downhill and into bushes. Iodine was eventually applied to the ensuing scrapes because there was no such thing as Neosporin.

In the afternoons, we went to the library and "borrowed" a new book, or we went swimmin' in the town pool. Evenings were filled with playing tag or other games and eating homemade ice cream.

Wistfully, I pine for a way back to the unworried summers of our youth, as the memories there are simply too delicious to forget.

August 7, 2008

Wisdom
of
Experience

Waiting for things to come full circle

Lessons in Respect

"Good morning, Mrs. Hausmann."

"Good morning, Mr. Hausmann."

Then, they shook hands. Such was the sweet daily morning ritual of a couple, both in their nineties, aunt and uncle of my hairdresser, Ann.

They were born and lived their entire lives in Germany.

You may wonder how Ann and I got on this subject of respectful morning greetings, but I'll get to that later.

The point is that the Hausmanns, both now deceased, began each day with respect for each other.

They shook hands. Think about it—shaking hands with your spouse when you first awaken!

As we know, however, few in this society show respect to strangers, let alone family.

Ann says she was raised that way in Germany, taught by example to shake hands with family and strangers alike.

Sadly, we admit that most of us do not tutor our offspring to show such reverence.

Fodder for another writing, no doubt, but for now, I have to wonder why this resonated so strongly with me.

The story she told reminded me of a Family Weekend we attended at the college of one of our sons.

Shortly after we arrived, our son introduced us to a new friend, Stephen, Stephen's parents, and his grandparents.

What did that entire family do but stand and shake our hands, and they did not sit down until we started to leave!

I have to confess I am not used to such wonderful manners except at business meetings.

Few people shake hands, let alone stand when you approach their table.

For the record, Stephen is a first-generation Korean American.

In his family, respect and good manners are as natural as our "How y'a doin'" Midwestern greeting.

Yet, one could not help but notice that such a greeting makes one feel better.

How awkward we Americans are at something as simple and effective as shaking hands and greeting others with kind deference.

I promised to say how Ann and I began discussing respect. Here's how it happened.

Ann is coloring my hair. She is making different strands stand out in diverse directions with three dissimilar colors, to be exact, when in walks her husband Peewee.

Don't be misled by his name.

Peewee is not a peewee. In fact, he is a strapping guy, retired Marine, toned and strong, even in his sixties.

Peewee comes in whistling, walks up to Ann and says, "Good Morning, Mrs. Woods."

He then shakes my hand and greets me.

Naturally, I can't stand up in my present state, covered with a cape and Ann working carefully on the intricacies of getting the color just right.

Peewee, who, by the way, is known for his sunny disposition, greets everyone in the salon and exits singing happily to himself.

I asked, "Is he always like this?"

Ann says yes, and that it is impossible to be grumpy around him, especially in the mornings.

She says she wants to be cranky lots of days, but when he greets her in such a manner, her bad temper melts away.

We could be onto something here.

In this country, the closest advice we have to holding others in high opinion is probably Aretha Franklin's.

Remember, she sang about it—R-E-S-P-E-C-T.

But, what if we all began shaking hands and treating those closest around us, as well as strangers, with good manners and admiration.

It's a heady thought.

Tom Ladwig, an old friend and veteran reporter, used to insist on simplicity in his writing as well as in life.

He had few bywords for life except these—remember to revere others, say "help me" in the morning and "thanks" at night, and in the meantime, remember to shake hands and smile. It is all coming back to me now.

"Good night, Mrs. Hausmann."

"Good night, Mr. Hausmann."

August 13, 2005

Words Will Be Used Against Us

Oh, how I wish I had not said that.

One must be very careful these days what one says to anyone, except maybe your dog.

There are lots of reasons to be careful.

If you happen to be running for political office, for instance, anything you say will be misquoted and used against you. You will look like a fool no matter what you say.

If you happen to encounter the "long arm of the law," you have the right to remain silent. Good idea to not put one's foot in one's mouth and just take your medicine.

If you are called in for a visit with a child's teacher, remember that children seldom misquote you. Darn. Instead, they usually repeat word for word what you should not have said.

Unlike running for office, you will get to hear your actual words played back exactly as you said them. It is as though children have a tape recorder in their brains.

Meanwhile, most of us adults of the aging variety would merely like to remember what we said or did not say.

Maybe we used to have photographic memories, but now we do not even have film. Wish I had said that myself, but I cannot remember, for the life of me, who did.

I suppose our memory difficulties do give us a bit of an excuse for saying foolish things out loud.

Thankfully, one can always count on the family pooch to listen carefully and not judge what silly pratter comes out of our mouths.

Dave Barry, famed humorist, understood my hypothesis completely when he commented, "You can say any foolish thing to a dog, and the dog will give you a look that says, 'My God, you are right! I never would have thought of that.'"

If you only have a cat around the house, your comments will be ignored with a yawn and a stretch. That is all you are going to get from the cat.

Let us take a tally so far: One must be very careful when we talk to the media, the police, or our children, but the dog and the cat are safe.

Is there anything else we need to consider before we open our mouths?

Actually, there is.

Political correctness, but I will not even go there.

I figure that as we age, we get a pass occasionally for our foolish remarks.

When we are fifty-five, people may frown when we say the wrong thing; at sixty, perhaps, one eyebrow will go up; and at sixty-five, one might see a twinkle in someone's eye. At seventy, our remarks could be received with a smile. At eighty, we can get away with anything because people just laugh and say, "Oh, isn't that cute."

Jenny Joseph said it best in her poem "Warning." Her famous poem, written in 1961, surmised that when she turns old she will wear purple, learn to spit, spend her pension on brandy and summer gloves, gobble up samples in shops, and sit on the pavement when she is tired.

As she noted, foolishness can be turned into gleeful defiance as one ages, but one does not need to wait on it.

Jenny added, "but maybe I ought to practise a little now? / So people who know me are not too shocked and surprised / When suddenly I am old, and start to wear purple."[43]

The same goes for fretting too much about our foolish remarks.

After this, I will say I am just practicing.

March 25, 2006

Some Days Nothing Goes Right

Some days there might as well be a warning message that flashes on my computer: "Smash head on keyboard to continue."

Days like that breed the blues. You know what it is like.

For starters, first thing Monday morning, the computer does not cooperate at all. Important letters get lost in the mail. Previously iron-clad contracts mysteriously fall apart. Phone messages get mixed up. Your loan payment gets applied to someone else's account. A deposit was not credited on time. A friend is mad at you and you have absolutely no idea what you did to incur their wrath. Travel tickets that you carefully mailed via overnight express to elderly relatives do not arrive as promised by 3:00 p.m. the next day. Of course, that is when they absolutely have to have them.

It is much like TV journalist Linda Ellerbee's philosophical lament, "And, so it goes."

By Sunday night you are positively worn out with it all. You have given up philosophizing about your distress, and that is when the blues begin to take hold. After all, Monday morning looms ominously on the horizon when all this fun will start all over again.

This is when I decide I must have the "Sunday Night Clanks," also known as the Sunday night blues. The act of diagnosing my ailment, in itself brings relief. Usually, I even manage a smile thinking about the "clanks."

Naturally, at this point one might rightly wonder why I call those blues the "clanks."

Many years ago, an old friend Pat first told me about the Sunday Night Clanks (SNC) when I was, admittedly, depressed and a tad whiney. I was convinced "the sky was falling." Today, I can't even remember why I was so miserable. Pat's explanation for my distress was soothing. Perhaps, just having a name for the malady helped.

Who knows? The point is that I began to feel better and laughed at such a silly name for my unhappy state of mind.

When my children were little, the Sunday night blues would cause them to worry and fret at bedtime. Their schoolwork was not finished. Their friends did not like them anymore. The teacher was mean. Worst of all, they did not get picked for the "cool" kids Four Square team during recess.

At that point, everything looked bleak and hopeless to them. This was my cue.

I would very confidently tell them that everything would be OK. The only thing wrong was that they had a bad case of the "Sunday Night Clanks." They never asked me what that was, come to think of it. They were satisfied with my answer and even smiled a bit. It might as well have been a Tuesday. They had a cause, a diagnosis, an explanation. That was good enough for them and off they went to bed. My grandmother had her own version of the SNC. She advised us, "When life brings problems to your door, do not worry and never, ever borrow trouble. It will all come out in the wash."

Calvin Coolidge said it another way, "Never go out to meet trouble. If you will just sit still, nine cases out of ten, someone will intercept it before it reaches you."

Don't worry. Be happy.

October 15, 2005

Note to Self: Save This

I adore saving snippets of wisdom and examples of colorful language, so much so that I keep a notebook full of them.

I save newspaper clippings with interesting words highlighted in yellow and scraps of paper with "notes to self" scribbled in the margins.

On my computer desktop, I have a folder entitled, "Interesting sayings to save."

Certainly, we all have our own little quirks and foibles. Apparently, this is one of mine, and for the record, I am keeping it.

Other people have their own peculiarities, too. For example, just the other day I read about some folks who are compulsive painters. They have repainted their living rooms six times and their bedroom, eight. They save paint swatches like I save words. They get up early or stay up late to repaint a hall, baseboards, ceiling, or furniture. A month or two later, they repaint it again.

My husband says they are losing square footage in their house by adding lots of layers of paint.

Not for me to judge, though, because my collection of sayings and words continues to grow.

Some years ago, I saved a column written by Barbara Shelly in the *Kansas City Star*. The headline caught my attention: "Flapdoodle discourse is on the move." Her commentary explained that a reader had once emailed her and advised, "Please tone down your inflammatory flapdoodle." She has used the word ever since.

I loved the word flapdoodle and now, finally have a place to use it—here!

Another scrap of scribbling I saved has to do with the difference between two French phrases, "*déjà vu*" and "*jaimais vu*." Most of us have heard of déjà vu, which means "already seen," but have you heard of *jaimais vu*? I had not.

Jaimais vu means when we stare at something familiar and have absolutely no recollection of it at all. Happens to me all the time. Someone says, "Oh, sure, you've seen that, you've been there," or "Surely, you remember that." I don't.

My old friend Tom Ladwig, journalism professor and author, cherished colorful words just like I do. Two of his favorites are saved on my computer: "widdershins" and "pettifogger."

I haven't found too many uses for these words, but they do roll off the tongue nicely and are fun to pronounce.

Widdershins means "in a contrary or counterclockwise direction."

Pettifogger means a petty, quibbling, unscrupulous lawyer, or one who quibbles over trivia.

It has come to my attention that lots of other people enjoy words, too.

Merriam-Webster Online conducted a search recently to find out the top ten favorite and most interesting words. You can bet I saved those.

Here's what they found out.

"Projects like this remind us once again of the deep level of interest that people attach to the words in their language," says John M. Morse, president and publisher of Merriam-Webster.

The No. 1 favorite word in their survey was "defenestration"—a throwing of a person or thing out of a window. I have to wonder why so many people even knew that word. Must be lots of people throwing things out of a window!

Serendipity came in No. 2, and onomatopoeia was No. 3. Finishing in the No. 10 spot was flibbertigibbet—meaning a silly, flighty person. Morse added, "Using language can be a little like serving up a meal, with words as the ingredients. I think people were sharing with us their favorite ingredients—the ingredients that add spice and flavor and a personal touch to their everyday use of language."

I understand exactly what Mr. Morse is saying and would only add this: "Although I have a plethora of aphorisms, I won't be persnickety about them and will not become discombobulated if they cause a kerfuffle."

October 22, 2005

The Best Gift on Mother's Day is to Take Her Advice

*"If at first you don't succeed, do it like your
mother told you in the first place."*

—UNKNOWN

Some of us are slow learners when it comes to heeding and understanding our mother's advice. In fact, it can take decades.

I know because I am sixty-one years old (I do not mind saying), and I am just now doing what my mother told me to do in 1969.

"Wear your cap and gown and go to your college graduation. You will regret it if you don't," my mother advised thirty-nine years ago.

Did I listen?

Of course not.

It was the '60s and wearing a cap and gown was "so establishment." Certainly, some graduates did listen to their mothers back then. However, at that point in time, I was headstrong, independent, and shall we say, too rebellious to pay attention.

My post-graduation employers, Ben and Ludmilla Weir of *The Examiner*, joined in my mother's chorus and told me to "walk across the stage" to receive my diploma rather than receive it by mail.

Once again, I did not listen.

As I said earlier, some of us are slow learners. But eventually, I came full circle.

This past weekend I had the honor and distinct pleasure of presenting a faculty award and making a short speech at a college commencement.

Imagine my déjà vu when I was told I would be wearing a cap and gown signifying the university where I graduated. The hood colors on the robe would designate my degree and field of study.

After thirty-nine years, I was finally walking across a college commencement stage wearing a cap and gown and could not have been happier about it.

I should have listened to my mother in the first place.

Therefore, my advice comes freely here and now to all prospective high school and college graduates: Don your cap and gown and do not miss your own commencement exercises.

Yes, the temperature inside a stuffy gymnasium will be hot. Yes, the speaker may be boring. Yes, the entire affair may seem juvenile to you. Yes, high school or college is already "so yesterday."

But a graduation ceremony will never seem silly or frivolous to your mother.

Taking her advice could be the best Mother's Day gift you could ever give her.

Note to moms: Give this story to offspring if you need ammo.

May 8, 2008

The Trouble with the Weather

"Weather is a great metaphor for life—
sometimes it's good, sometimes it's bad,
and there's nothing much you can do about it
but carry an umbrella or choose to dance in the rain."[44]

—TERRI GUILLEMETS,
creator of the Quote Garden

The trouble with the weather right now in the Midwest is that we can't make the rain stop.

Anyone know a reverse rain dance?

I found one blogger named Angela who said she caused a California water shortage by doing the Hokey Pokey, and I think she believes she did.

Somehow, I don't think the Hokey Pokey will help in Missouri, as we face record flooding this spring and a punch in the face from tornadoes, hail, wild thunder and lightning storms, and rain, seemingly endless rain.

Regardless of whether you love or hate these storms, one has to agree that spring storms are hypnotic, frightening, captivating, spellbinding, powerful, and magnetic.

They are both our friend and foe.

Lisa Fritscher, online health journalist, explains that storms are natural occurrences that tend to illicit strong emotions in both humans and animals, even though nature tends to make things right in the end. In fact, some people have such strong reactions to storms that they develop a condition known as astraphobia, the fear of thunder and lightning storms.

It is difficult to imagine how floods, tornados, and lightning could be good for us, especially if one happens to be afraid of storms.

For most of us, I guess you could say that we love storms or hate them, but mostly, we do not understand them. We do love to watch them, however.

Which type of weather watcher are you, incidentally?

One who is obsessed with the weather channel and tracking storms online and won't go outside without checking these first?

One who does not take storms seriously at all and is not afraid of any old lightening in the distance? This type might stand on a metal ladder during a lightning storm because he or she needs to finish cleaning out the gutters and the job can't wait.

A thrill seeker who delights in lightning crashes, the nearer the better?

An artist who wants to make videos or take photographs of violent but beautiful skies?

A fun lover who dances in the rain and jumps in puddles?

Those who simply enjoy the quiet solitude of watching storms, in awe of the spectacular power of nature?

With these thoughts in mind, here's a little weather quiz for you. See if you can find yourself in the list below of strong emotional reactions to storms and how you score.

- Do you hate the loud, booming burst of noise, that first clap of thunder, so much that you cover your ears?
- Do you run for the basement?
- Hide under the covers?
- Call out for your mother?
- Are you more afraid than your dog?
- Are you pessimistic enough about storms that you believe the number one reason tornado season is like Christmas is that sooner or later you are going to have a tree in your house?

If you answered "yes" to more than three of these, don't worry. You may just need some old-fashioned homespun advice from my favorite coffee shop weather gurus.

Such as, "Sweetie, I'm sure the rain is scared of you, too."

Or, "For crying out loud, why don't you move to Arizona where it hasn't rained in hundreds of years?"

"Come on, it's not going to flood. You live on a hill."

"Do you remember the movie *Back to the Future*? In the film, Doc explained that his invention, a 'flux capacitor,' could harness a lightning bolt made up of 1.21 'jigowatts' of power and propel a time machine back to 1955. Lightning is a powerful source of energy. Think about it."

Think "flux capacitor." Yup, that advice could be the best I've heard yet.

Next time lightning strips the bark from the locust tree in the backyard and the cow in the field across the creek moos so loudly it wakes the neighborhood, yessirree, I will think "flux capacitor" and feel ever so much better.

Oh, the trouble with weather indeed.

April 28, 2011

Typing is like Riding a Bike—
We Never Forget How

"It's like riding a bicycle or typing. If you are willing to work at it, you can rapidly improve the quality of every part of your life."

—**BRIAN TRACY**, author and inspirational speaker

It was the 1960s and that is when I learned to type, by rote.

My teacher, the late Miss Jenny Ellen Cardinell, would have it no other way. (She was actually married, but back then nearly all female teachers were addressed as "Miss").

Learning to type in Miss Cardinell's class was a mechanical course of procedure, fixed and without thought of the meaning. "One must practice and learn by repetition," she would say.

She was right. Once one knows how, one never forgets.

We may get rusty, but we always know how to type. Just like riding a bike.

For instance, if someone asked you to type a practice phrase on a computer these days, what would you type?

If you are of a certain age, I am betting that you would type this sentence without thinking about it: "Now is the time for all good men to come to the aid of their country."

In my high school typing classes, and no doubt many of yours, students practiced typing by producing pages and pages of such phrases and completing exercises that emphasized mastery of punctuation and numbers. And most importantly, where the letters and numbers were located on the keyboard.

We became highly proficient at the typing method known as QWERTY.

QWERTY is the universal nomenclature for a typewriter keyboard and comes from the first six letters in the top alphabet row, the one just below the numbers, and the configuration spells "QWERTY."

We probably learned that definition at the time, but if you were like me, it really didn't sink in much.

We also learned the history of the typewriter, which we promptly forgot.

Such as, C.L. Sholes was the inventor who first built a model keyboard in his machine shop in Milwaukee in the 1860s. And later, a certain pattern of keys was introduced on the "Type Writer" in 1872, a clumsy device by today's standards.

That original keyboard was designed to improve speed by determining frequency of letter pairing.

Decades later, in 1978, Remington Company, an arms manufacturer, made the only major modification to QWERTY—adding a shift key.

Few changes have been made since to keyboards. Amazingly, they got it right from the outset.

And so did our typing teachers who taught us much about life when all we thought we were learning was how to type.

We learned to be accurate, work quickly, correct our mistakes at once, and to never do sloppy or shoddy work.

We learned to commit to mind, soul, and heart the first words we ever learned to type: "Now is the time for all good men to come to the aid of their country."

It occurred to me how relevant that simple typing exercise is today. Perhaps in this crazy world of ours if we practiced what we learned in typing classes so many years ago, the world might be better for it.

So, I have resolved to type that phrase more often and to remember its advice in the days ahead.

The easy part is I already "know" it by heart.

September 23, 2010

Waiting for Things to Come Full Circle

It's funny how things come full circle in life, and it is always serendipitous and surprising when it happens.

Such as an old friend Marilyn and her lost recipe for lime pickles that showed up for me just in the nick of time.

I guess that is why I named this column "Full Circle" in the first place, because I find it fascinating and incredibly entertaining when such things happen, no matter how small or seemingly insignificant.

But now, here's the backstory of how this lost lime pickle recipe took a rather circuitous path and came full circle through Facebook and a radio talk show to my recipe file.

Marilyn entrusted me with her secret recipe sometime in the summer of 1981, if I remember correctly. Shortly thereafter, I promptly copied and shared it with friends, made canned pickles to give as Christmas gifts offered in pint jars with ribbons and a copy of the recipe attached, and I even included the recipe in my Christmas letter. I don't think Marilyn minded much.

Yet, somehow, despite its extensive distribution, I lost it.

After twenty-eight years, this highly coveted, envied, and long since forgotten recipe showed up just in time for August canning.

More importantly, it came 'round just in time to be added to a cherished collection of family recipes as a gift for my son's upcoming wedding. The acute problem for me was that I lost it years ago, and I could not find it anywhere with the wedding fast approaching.

Now, August arrives when the cucumbers are profuse and begging to be canned and the aforementioned wedding is mere weeks away and only Marilyn's recipe will do.

Enter Facebook and a radio station.

Over that weekend I noticed on Facebook that my niece-in-law Elizabeth wrote on my wall that her mother Karen listened to a radio talk show program in which my old friend Marilyn was the honored guest. The program was a spot titled *Keeping Good Company* and featured an interesting, accomplished community resident (Marilyn) who has contributed much to the area throughout a lifetime.

The station in question is KWRT 1370 AM in Boonville, Missouri, and turns out that one of the DJs is Sharon, a fellow Mizzou Journalism School alum.

Sharon interviewed Marilyn, who talked about the fun we had in the '80s when she was an advertising salesman at my old newspaper/shopper, *The Penny Post*, in Boonville. Marilyn also discussed some of her favorite recipes, however, she did not mention her famous one for lime pickles. In true Marilyn style, she brought along her also-famous jalapeño pie concoction for the DJs to taste. For the record, all of Marilyn's recipes are "famous" or should be.

Are you following this okay so far?

Elizabeth posted the story on Facebook about how Sharon interviewed Marilyn on the radio and they both reminisced about my weekly newspaper and recipes. I then searched and found Sharon on Facebook so she could fill in the gaps in the story.

It was then, and only then, the thought occurred to me that if I looked in the basement in one of my storied boxes of life memorabilia that reside in the bowels of this edifice that I might find copies of my old *Penny Post* newspaper. I knew they were there somewhere. Sure enough, there was the lime pickle recipe printed in a food section in August of 1981.

But it took a radio interview and a Facebook post to jog my memory enough to help me look in the right box in the basement.

And that's why I like things coming full circle, which they almost always do. You never know what's coming next. Our only challenge is to wait for them.

CRISP CUCUMBER LIME PICKLES

7 lbs. cucumbers peeled and cut to thumb-size pieces
2 cups hydrated lime
2 gallons water

Cover cukes with lime water solution. Let stand 24 hours. Take cukes out of solution, rinse thoroughly, and cover with clear cold water. Let stand 3 hours. Drain water off cukes, cover with the following ingredients, and let stand overnight.

1½ quarts vinegar
2 tsp. cloves, whole
2 tsp. celery seed
2 tsp. pickling spice
1 T. coarse salt
4½ lbs. sugar or 9 cups

After standing overnight, boil cucumbers in mixture for 35 minutes. Add ¾ to 1 teaspoon green food coloring when cukes first start to boil. Put in hot jars and seal while liquid is hot. Makes 8 to 9 pints. Double recipe yields only about 10 quarts.

August 6, 2009

Acknowledgments

This book would not have been possible without the trust and vision of two experienced editors.

Sheila Davis, executive editor, now retired, of the *The Examiner*, a daily Missouri newspaper, and Dale Brendel, former general manager of *The Examiner* and later publisher of *The Joplin Globe*. They took a chance on me when I pitched them five sample columns, none of which were particularly good, in my humble opinion. Sheila and Dale took me to lunch, and we talked about what the column could entail. Seven years of weekly newspaper columns followed until the day I officially retired. I greatly appreciate their counsel and support.

Editors Andrea Rice and Nan Bauroth, at different times and for different reasons, patiently read, analyzed, and organized three hundred-plus columns for possible inclusion in this book. Each, in their own way, helped me think through and see "the big picture" of what I wanted this book to be. Thank you both. I am indebted.

And special thanks to the publishing team at Brown Books Publishing Group of Dallas, Texas. Thank you for your guidance, encouragement, and confidence that started from the first day I spoke to Thomas Reale, president and COO. Tom and crew applied exactly the right amount of pressure to move me along toward my deadlines and keep me smiling along the way. It's a journey, and I will remain grateful to them for their leadership. Incidentally, today Brown Books Publishing Group is recognized as one of the most successful independent publishing houses in the country. It's a major publisher that allows authors like me to be directly involved in the publication of their work and to retain rights to it. I like that mix.

And lastly, a heartfelt and huge thank you to my big and boisterous family and dear friends, old and new, who provided fodder for my newspaper stories each week and endless support for this writing adventure. Thankfully, they didn't seem to mind, too awfully much, when I wrote about them.

As my Dad used to say, "This puts me in the mind of another story." It puts me in the mind of this quote from Mae West: "I always say, keep a diary, and someday it will keep you." (Note to Generations X, Y, and Z—you may need to look that one up.)

Kay Hoflander

Notes

1. *The Bridges of Madison County*, directed by Clint Eastwood (Madison County, Iowa: Warner Brothers, 1995), DVD.
2. Christine Dell'amore, "To Stave Off Alzheimer's, Learn a Second Language?" *National Geographic Magazine*, February 18, 2011, https://www.nationalgeographic.com/culture/article/100218-bilingual-brains-alzheimers-dementia-science-aging
3. Ellen Bialystok, "Bilingualism as a Protection Against the Onset of Symptoms of Dementia," *Neuropsychologia* 45 (November 2006): 459–464, doi:10.1016/j.neuropsychologia.2006.10.009 (yorku.ca).
4. *Fox and Friends*, aired in April 2009, on Fox.
5. *Boston Legal*, created by David E. Kelley, aired 2004–2008.
6. A A Milne and Joan Powers, *Pooh's Little Instruction Book* (New York City: Dutton, 1995).
7. *Just You and Me, Kid*, directed by Leonard Stern (Los Angeles and Van Nuys, California: Columbia Pictures, 1979), DVD.
8. David Crary, "Boomers Seek to Define Legacy," CBS News, December 12, 2005, https://www.cbsnews.com/news/boomers-seek-to-define-legacy/.
9. Ron Kovic, *Born on the Fourth of July* (New York City: McGraw Hill, 1976).
10. Nora Ephron, *I Remember Nothing* (New York City: Knopf Doubleday Publishing Group, 2010).
11. E. B. White, *The Second Tree From the Corner* (New York City: Harper & Bros., 1954).
12. James Doyle, "Vitamins," https://judithpordon.tripod.com/poetry/james_doyle_vitamins.html.
13. Tom Rush, "Remember Song," written by Steven Walters, live performance, March 1, 2007, https://www.youtube.com/watch?v=9yN-6PbqAPM.

14. Ibid.

15. *Ferris Bueller's Day Off*, directed by John Hughes (Chicago: Paramount Pictures, 1986), DVD.

16. Dr. Seuss, *Oh, the Places You'll Go!* (New York City: Penguin Random House, 1990).

17. "Memorial Day 1999 Speech" (speech), US Memorial Day (website), 1999, transcript, https://www.usmemorialday.org/memorial-day-1999-speech.

18. Tom Brokaw, *The Greatest Generation* (New York City: Penguin Random House, 1998).

19. Winston Churchill, "Liberation of Rome: Landings in France" (speech), June 6, 1944, UK Parliament API, transcript, https://api.parliament.uk/historic-hansard/commons/1944/jun/06/liberation-of-rome-landings-in-france#S5CV0400P0_19440606_HOC_230.

20. Gen. Dwight Eisenhower, "Order of the Day" (letter), US Government Archives, 1944, transcript and image, ww2-eisenhower-d-day-order.pdf (archives.gov).

21. Rita Mae Brown, *Starting From Scratch: A Different Kind of Writers' Manual* (New York City: Penguin Random House, 1989).

22. Paula Ford-Martin, "Types of Dementia," WebMD (website), medically reviewed by Jennifer Casarella, MD, September 29, 2020, https://www.webmd.com/alzheimers/guide/alzheimers-dementia.

23. Arthur C. Clarke, *Profiles of the Future*, rev. ed. (New York City: Harper & Row, 1973).

24. *I Dream of Jeannie*, created by Sidney Sheldon, aired 1965-1970, on NBC.

25. *Siri*, iPhone ed., (Apple, 2010). iOS 4 or later.

26. Ibid.

27. *I Dream of Jeannie*, created by Sidney Sheldon, aired 1965-1970, on NBC.

28. *Siri*, iPhone ed., (Apple, 2010). iOS 4 or later.

29. Anna North, "The GPS Lady Could Destroy Your Relationship," Jezebel (website), June 25, 2010, https://jezebel.com/the-gps-lady-could-destroy-your-relationship-5572946.

30. Bruce Feiler, "Turn Right, My Love," *New York Times*, June 27, 2010, https://www.nytimes.com/2010/06/27/fashion/27Family-Matters.html?partner=rss&emc=rss.

31. Sydney, Six-Word Memoirs (website), August 18, 2008, https://www.sixwordmemoirs.com/story/?did=29549.

32. Zuleika, Six-Word Memoirs (website), July 12, 2009, https://www.sixwordmemoirs.com/story/?did=70504.

33. PantsMacKenzie, Six-Word Memoirs (website), July 12, 2009, https://www.sixwordmemoirs.com/story/?did=70528.

34. Theresa Knapp, "Medfield's 'Computer Mom' Keeps Systems Running Virus Free," *Medfield Press*, December 28, 2010, https://www.wickedlocal.com/story/thepress/2010/12/29/medfield-s-computer-mom-keeps/39222167007/.

35. Glen Levy, "Legally #Winning: Charlie Sheen Wants to Trademark 22 Catchphrases," *Time*, April 6, 2011, https://newsfeed.time.com/2011/04/06/financially-winning-charlie-sheen-wants-to-trademark-22-catchphrases/.

36. Chloe Albanesius, "Tiger Blood and Winning: Charlie Sheen Joins Twitter," PC Magazine, March 2, 2011, https://uk.pcmag.com/news/104337/tiger-blood-and-winning-charlie-sheen-joins-twitter.

37. Miley Cyrus (@MileyCyrus), "I'm not gonna lie. I came back to Twitter for two reasons: My fans and to follow @charliesheen #winning," Twitter, April 3, 2011, 5:24 p.m., https://twitter.com/MileyCyrus/status/54670570926768129.

38. Shigeru Matsushima, "Japan's Cell Phone Novels Dominate Bestseller List," The Mercury News, January 19, 2008, https://www.mercurynews.com/2008/01/19/japans-cell-phone-novels-dominate-bestseller-list/.

39. Norimitsu Onishi, "Thumbs Race as Japan's Best Sellers Go Cellular," *New York Times*, January 20, 2008, https://www.nytimes.com/2008/01/20/world/asia/20japan.html?searchResultPosition=1.

40. Ibid.

41. Laurie Colwin, *Gourmet*, 1992.

42. "The Best Thing to Get Out of Marriage Is to Get Out of Marriage–Guests Audrey Meadows, Ted Mack, The Lettermen," *The Red Skeleton Hour*, aired January 14, 1969, on NBC.

43. Jenny Joseph, *Rose in the Afternoon and Other Poems* (Dent, 1974).

44. Terri Guillemets, The Quote Garden (website), originally written December 19, 1991, https://www.quotegarden.com/weather.html.

About the Author

Kay Hoflander holds a bachelor's degree in journalism from the University of Missouri-Columbia and has worked as a daily newspaper reporter and editor, freelance writer, and publisher of a biweekly newspaper-shopper. She loves writing, volunteerism, and politics.

Kay and her husband live in rural Missouri and are the parents of five children and the grandparents of ten grandchildren. Their big, boisterous, and lively family enjoys spending time together at the Lake of the Ozarks and in the Colorado Mountains.

About the Illustrator

Scot Ritchie is an award-winning illustrator and author. His books have been translated into languages including French, Korean, Chinese, Finnish, Arabic, and Dutch.

He has worked with the National Film Board of Canada and had his illustrations exhibited at the National Gallery of Canada. Scot mostly writes and illustrates books, but he also enjoys the wild world of editorial illustration and cartoons (maybe they're the flip side of kids' books.)

As a freelancer, Scot has been able to pack up his office and work in cities like Athens, Berlin, and Honolulu. He stays for a few months, convincing himself (he's quite impressionable) that he lives there. He actually lives in Vancouver.